Herbert Puchta
G. Gerngross C. Hol...

MORE! 4

Student's Book

MAP OF THE BOOK

	Grammar	Language Focus and Vocabulary	Skills	MORE!
UNIT 1 Football? Soccer?	• present simple, present continuous and present perfect	• sports clothes **Sounds right** /s/ vs /z/	• chat on the phone • buy things in a sports shop • read about unusual British sports • listen to an American's trip to a UK football match • talk and write about a memorable sporting occasion	**Learn MORE through English** Early US history History
UNIT 2 Space and beyond	• past continuous vs past simple • past perfect • narrative tenses (Revision)	• travel	• give reasons • talk about your journey to school • listen and find out about *A race to space* • listen to a poem • talk about and write a short sci-fi story	**Check your progress** Units 1 and 2 **Learn MORE about culture** Trains planes and automobiles! **Read MORE for pleasure** Alien worlds
UNIT 3 Shopping	• should(n't) / ought (n't) • gerunds	• money and shopping **Sounds right** Spelling	• say what people ought to do • talk about shopping • read a quiz and talk about your shopping habits • read and listen to find out about *Buy Nothing Day* • write a letter to help someone with a money problem	**Learn MORE through English** Space travel Science
UNIT 4 A working life	• be going to + present continuous (Revision) • future time clauses	• personality adjectives	• say what you want to do • talk about jobs and personality • read about a foreign girl living and working in the UK • listen to two people talking about their job interviews • write a description of someone's job	**Check your progress** Units 3 and 4 **Learn MORE about culture** Beefeaters! **Read MORE for pleasure** Omelettes and hard work
UNIT 5 Bookworms	• so / such • phrasal verbs	• types of books **Sounds right** Stress in compound nouns	• give reasons • talk about books • read about the Alex Rider books • listen to teens talking about reading • talk and write about a book you enjoyed	**Learn MORE through English** Migration Biology
UNIT 6 The main event	• the passive • make / let / be allowed to	• special events	• talking about events • talking about permission • read about events in Rio de Janeiro • listen to some facts about Wimbledon • talk about organising a charity event and design a poster for it	**Check your progress** Units 5 and 6 **Learn MORE about culture** Marathons! **Read MORE for pleasure** Chill out at the Guilfest

2

	Grammar	Language Focus and Vocabulary	Skills	MORE!
UNIT 7 Food, glorious food	• *will / won't* predictions • question tags (Revision)	• food **Sounds right** Question intonation	• talk about food • make offers • read about a campaign for healthier food in British schools • talk about what food you like • listen to a radio report on Britain's least healthy cities • write about your eating habits	Learn **MORE** through English Musical styles Music
UNIT 8 Body talk	• *could, might, may* for speculation • *-ed* vs *-ing* adjectives	• body movements	• talk about emotions • talk about body movements • read about the history of body piercing • listen to a synopsis of the film *Fantastic Voyage* • write a film review	**Check your progress** Units 7 and 8 Learn **MORE** about culture Street performers Read **MORE** for pleasure It must be her age
UNIT 9 Fame	• *used to* (Revision) • gerunds after prepositions	• award shows **Sounds right** Questions	• talk about past and present favourites • talk about awards • read about fame and happiness • listen to someone talk about their favourite star • talk and write about someone you admire • listen to the song *Fame*	Learn **MORE** through English The city of Vancouver Geography
UNIT 10 Crazy collectors	• present perfect continuous • embedded questions	• hobbies and pastimes	• talk about hobbies • talk about collecting something • listen to someone talking about their collection • read about people with unusual collections • talk and write about collecting things	**Check your progress** Units 9 and 10 Learn **MORE** about culture Unusual collections Read **MORE** for pleasure Britain's biggest egg collector
UNIT 11 Speak out	• reported speech • reported questions	• personality adjectives **Sounds right** Reporting direct speech	• check what people do / explain what you do • describe people • read a poem called *Me* • listen to teens talking about young people • talk about young people and their problems • read and write a letter to a problem page	Learn **MORE** through English Understanding poetry English
UNIT 12 A fair world?	• *if*-clauses (Revision)	• work places	• talk about what you would have done • talk about places • listen to stories about people who got into trouble • read a diary entry about an unfair situation and then write your own • discuss unfair situations and how you would react	**Check your progress** Units 11 and 12 Learn **MORE** about culture Ethical buying! Read **MORE** for pleasure Fair? Well …

Word list

MAP OF THE BOOK

UNIT 1 Football? Soccer?

In this unit

You learn
- present simple
- present continuous
- present perfect (Revision)
- words for sports clothes

and then you can
- chat on the phone
- buy things in a sports shop

1 Listen and read.

Emily Asher! Hi. What are you doing here?

Asher Hi Emily. I'm waiting for Pete. We're going to the match together.

Emily Oh, right. By the way, this is my friend Greg.

Asher Hi Greg. How are you?

Greg Hey Asher. Fine thanks, and you?

Asher Yeah, fine. So, you're not from England, are you?

Greg No, I'm from the States. We live in Boston, but my dad's working in the UK for a year, so — here we are.

Emily Greg's living in the house next door to us. He's only been in England for two weeks.

Greg That's right. There's a lot to learn — some things are really different here! I mean — what's in your bag? And what are those things?

Asher These are batting gloves. You wear them when you play cricket. Have you heard of cricket?

Greg I think so. It's a sport that you guys play in the summer.

Asher That's right. I love it. I'm not very good, though.

Emily It's a bit like baseball.

Asher Well, no, not really — but never mind! But, listen, Greg — do you play football?

Greg Absolutely. I've played football since I was six years old. I'm a quarterback.

Asher A what? Ah — I get it. Sorry, I'm not talking about American football — I'm talking about our football.

Greg Right — soccer. No, I've never played it — but I'd love to try. Are you in a team?

Emily OK you two. That's enough about sport. Can we talk about something else, please?

2 Correct the wrong information in each sentence.

1 Asher is waiting for Emily. — No — Asher is waiting for Pete.
2 Greg's dad is working in Boston for a year.
3 Greg has been in England for a month.
4 Greg has seen cricket gloves before.
5 Asher is very good at cricket.
6 Asher thinks cricket is a bit like baseball.
7 Greg has never played American football.
8 Emily wants to talk more about sport.

Get talking Chatting on the phone

3 Listen to the dialogues. Then read the texts and match them with the pictures.

1 Girl Hello Steve. What are you doing?
Boy Hi Sally. I'm doing my homework. And you?
Girl I'm not doing anything.

2 Boy What are you doing, Monica?
Girl I'm writing an email to my friend in America.

3 Girl Hello Andy. What are you doing?
Boy Hey Joanna. I'm waiting for the bus. And you?
Girl I'm buying new clothes for the party on Saturday.

4 Work with a partner. Make conversations like the ones in Exercise 3. Use the pictures.

Language Focus

Vocabulary Sports clothes

1 Match the words and pictures. Then listen and check.

- [ ] gloves
- [ ] shirt
- [ ] helmet
- [ ] boots
- [ ] pads
- [ ] vest
- [ ] shorts
- [ ] socks
- [ ] goggles
- [ ] trainers

   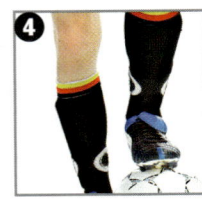 

2 Answer the questions about the sports clothes in Exercise 1.

1 For which things do we say 'a pair of .....'?
2 Which of the things do people wear when they:
   a) go skateboarding?   c) go cycling?   e) play tennis?
   b) play football?   d) go running?

> When people play ......, they wear boots / a shirt / knee pads / a helmet (etc.)

Get talking Buying things in a sports shop

3 Number the dialogue in the correct order. Listen and check.

...... 6, I think.
..1.. Can I help you?
...... Oh, they look fine. Can I try them on, please?
...... OK. What size do you take?
...... Sure – go ahead.
...... Well, we've got these.
...... Yes. I need a pair of rugby boots.

4 Work with partner. Make similar conversations about:

- a football shirt
- a running vest
- a pair of trainers
- a pair of cycling shorts

6 UNIT 1

Grammar

Present simple / Present continuous / Present perfect (Revision)

1 Look at the sentences and write the name of the correct tense PS (Present simple), PC (Present continuous) and PP (Present perfect).

1 **Do** you **play** football? ....
2 **Have** you **heard** of cricket? ....
3 He**'s been** in England for two weeks. ....
4 He**'s living** in the house next door. ....
5 I **don't play** very well. ....
6 I**'m** not **talking** about American football. ....
7 I**'ve** never **played** it. ....
8 We **live** in Boston. ....
9 What **are** you **doing** here? ....

2 Match the questions and answers.

1 Do you like tennis?
2 What are you doing?
3 Have you finished your homework?
4 What time do you go to school?
5 Do you like banana ice cream?
6 Has Sandra sent you an email?
7 Have you ever been to the USA?
8 What are you reading?

a) At eight o'clock.
b) Yes, but I don't play it very well.
c) Yes, I'm opening it now.
d) No, but I want to go one day.
e) I'm writing an email to Johnny.
f) A book about Boston.
g) No. I'm still doing it.
h) I don't know. I've never eaten it.

3 Circle the correct form of the verb.

1 **A** Where's Pauline?
   B She's in her room. *She's talking / She talks* to her friend on the phone.
2 **A** Are you a good skater?
   B Yes, I am. *I go / I'm going* skating every weekend.
3 **A** Can I talk to you, please?
   B Not now – *I'm watching / I've watched* a TV programme. Let's talk later.
4 **A** What's the matter?
   B I can't find my pen. *Have you seen / Are you seeing* it?
5 **A** She likes magazines.
   B Yes. *She reads / She's reading* every day.
6 **A** Is that a good book?
   B I don't know – *I don't read / I haven't read* it.

UNIT 1

4 Match the sentences and the pictures.

1 Paula plays the guitar.
2 Paula's playing the guitar.
3 Alan's talking on the phone.
4 Alan talks a lot on the phone.
5 Our cat chases birds.
6 Our cat is chasing birds.
7 She sings really well.
8 She's singing really well tonight.

5 Complete the sentences with the Present simple or the Present continuous form of the verbs.

1 Sorry, I can't talk to you now – I *'m having* dinner. (have)
2 In my house, we .... dinner at half past eight. (have)
3 My father .... home for work at 7.30 every day. (leave)
4 Shhh! I .... television. (watch)
5 Do you know where Graham is? I .... for him. (look)
6 **A** I play tennis with Sally every Saturday. **B** Really? Who ....? (win)
7 **A** The football match started twenty minutes ago. **B** Oh? Who ....? (win)

6 Circle the correct verb.

1 Here's the money! I *find / 've found* it!
2 We *live / have lived* in this house for ten years.
3 Jane's ill – she *doesn't go / hasn't been* to school for three days.
4 My parents are never here on Sunday afternoon – they *visit / have visited* my grandparents.
5 I don't know what happens in the film – I *don't see / haven't seen* it.

7 Complete the sentences with the Present perfect simple of the verbs.

1 Sorry, he isn't here – he *'s gone* out. (go)
2 I .... never .... to go to America. (want)
3 I .... a new pair of trainers – do you like them? (buy)
4 .... you .... their new CD? (hear)
5 Our teacher .... us lots of homework for tonight. (give)
6 There are no apples left – you .... them all! (eat)
7 We're still waiting for the bus – it .... yet. (not come)
8 He's nervous because he .... for the exam. (not study)

8   UNIT 1

Skills

Reading and speaking

1 Read the texts. Match each text to a photo.

A   B   C

Only in the UK – Unusual British sports

1 Bog snorkelling
If you have a snorkel and a pair of flippers you could take part in a very unusual sport – bog snorkelling. The first world championships took place in 1985 and ever since that year competitors have come to Llanwrtyd Wells in Wales to take part in this strange event. So what do you have to do? Well, a bog is like a very narrow river filled with muddy water. To win the bog snorkelling title you have to swim about 60m up and 60m back down a very cold and dirty bog faster than anyone else.

2 Conkers
The game of conkers has been popular with British school children for more than 150 years. Conkers are the hard seeds from the horse chestnut tree. In a game of conkers both players tie their conkers to the end of a piece of string. Players then take turns to hit their opponent's conker. If your conker breaks, you lose. In 1965, the first world championship was held in Ashton, England. These days competitors come from all over the world to take part.

3 Cheese rolling
Every year in May in the Cotswold region of England, hundreds of people turn up to take part in the Cooper hill cheese rolling competition. The rules are simple. A large round Double Gloucester cheese is rolled down the steep hill and all the competitors then chase after it. The first person to cross the finish line wins the cheese. However, this is not a sport for the weak and most years at least one person ends up in hospital with a broken leg.

2 Read these sentences. Which sport is each sentence about?

1. It's quite a dangerous sport.
2. It's popular with children.
3. You need to be a good swimmer.
4. It's popular in other countries.
5. The winner gets food.

3 Discuss in small groups.

1. Do you consider these to be sports? Why/why not?
2. Which one would you like to take part in most? Why?
3. What strange sports do you know of in your country?

UNIT 1   9

Listening

 4 **Listen to an American boy talking about his trip to an English football game. Answer these questions.**

1 Which city was Sam in?
2 Which two teams were playing?
3 Which team won?

 5 **Listen again. Decide if the sentences below are T (True) or F (False).**

1 Manchester United play at Old Trafford.   T / F
2 The weather was quite warm.   T / F
3 The game started at 6 pm.   T / F
4 Sam thought the stadium was small.   T / F
5 Sam tried to sing along with the fans.   T / F
6 Sam thought the hotdogs were ok.   T / F
7 Manchester United won the game 3 - 2.   T / F
8 Sam really enjoyed the evening.   T / F

Speaking

6 **Choose a sentence for each photo. Compare your answers with a partner and explain your reasons.**

1 Everyone had a great time.
2 We won!
3 It was really exciting.
4 The noise was incredible.
5 It was just for fun.
6 There were so many people there!
7 It was a really important match.
8 We lost but it didn't matter.

7 **Tell your partner about a memorable sporting occasion.**

Writing for your Portfolio

8 Complete Roberto's text with the words on the left.

country
wait
together
painted
unfortunately
interested
windows
sad

Three years ago it was the World Cup. I'm not really very ¹ ……………… in football but the other people in my family really love it. So we had a good time when we sat down ² ……………… and watched the games on TV – especially when our ³ ……………… played!
We were very excited when our country got to the semi-final. And people in our city went crazy too! They put flags in the ⁴ ……………… of their houses, and people wore shirts with the team colours – and on the day of the match, lots of people ⁵ ……………… their faces, too. It was brilliant!
We went to our neighbours' house to watch the semi-final – it started at 8 o'clock at night. The match was quite exciting, but ⁶ ………………, we lost 2-1!
So we were all a bit ⁷ ………………, but it didn't matter very much because we all had a good time.
Now I can't ⁸ ……………… for the next World Cup – it's next year!

9 Read the text again and answer the questions.

1. Which sport is the story about?
2. What did people put in the windows of their houses?
3. What did people do to their faces?
4. Where did Roberto watch the semi-final?
5. Who won the match?
6. What is Roberto looking forward to?

10 Write a text entitled *A sports event I remember*.

1. Was it a sporting event that you took part in or watched?
2. Where was the event? Or where did you watch it?
3. Who else was there?
4. What was the atmosphere like?
5. What were your expectations?
6. What happened?
7. How did you feel about it?
8. Why do you still remember this occasion?

Sounds right /s/ vs /z/

11 Listen to some of the words from Exercise 1, page 6. Decide which end with an /s/ sound and which with a /z/ sound.

/s/	/z/

UNIT 1

Early US history

Key words

belief	harvest	turkey	tax
successful	native	colony	merchants
fight	corn	independent	harbour

1 Read the article about the Pilgrims. Match the questions and the paragraphs.

a) What happened when they got to America?
b) How do Americans remember them?
c) Who were they?
d) Why did they go to America?
e) How and when did they go to America?

THE PILGRIMS

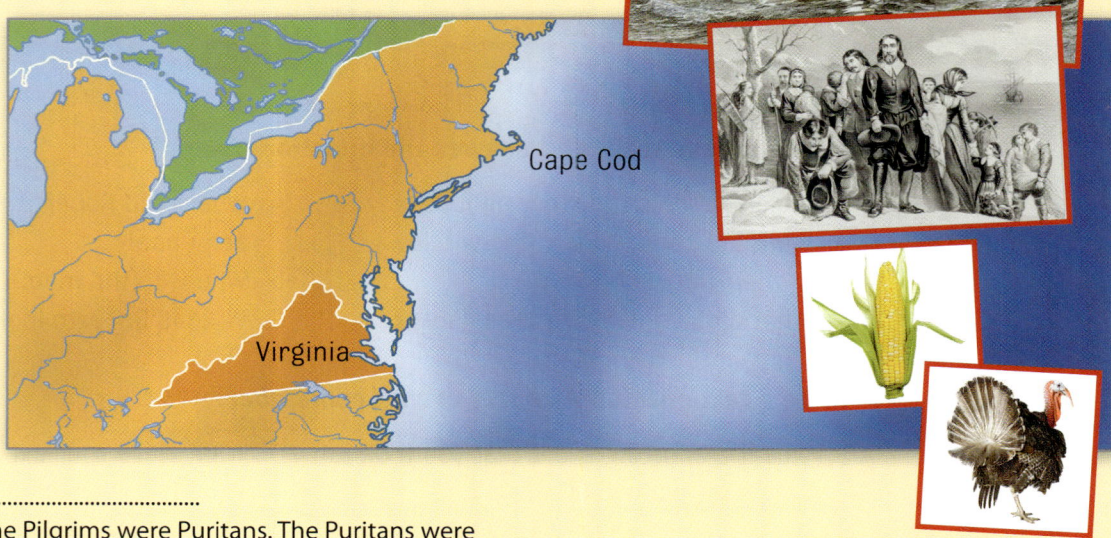

1 ....
The Pilgrims were Puritans. The Puritans were people who lived in England in the 16th and 17th centuries. Many people didn't like them because their beliefs were very different. A lot of Puritans went to live in Holland, but they weren't very happy there, either.

2 ....
People thought that America (the 'New World') was a place where they could be rich and happy – a place where they could live as they wanted. So some Puritans decided to go to America.

3 ....
On the 5th of August, 1620, 101 Pilgrims went to America in a ship called *The Mayflower*. They left Southampton and began a six-week journey to the New World. Many people died on the journey.

4 ....
The Pilgrims did not have enough food. But they were lucky because friendly native Americans showed them how to hunt animals, how to make sugar, and how to grow corn. The Pilgrims also found a strange bird that they could eat – the turkey.

5 ....
In the autumn of 1621, the Pilgrims had their first successful harvest. To say 'Thank You', they gave themselves a holiday and had a special meal with turkey. This was the first Thanksgiving. In 1863, Thanksgiving became a national holiday in the USA. It is celebrated on the fourth Thursday in November every year. Thanksgiving dinner usually has roast turkey.

2 **What do you know about the Boston Tea Party? Decide whether the statements below are T (True) or F (False).**

1 In the 1700s, Boston was a small port. T / F
2 In 1770 America was still a colony of Britain. T / F
3 Americans had to pay taxes to Britain. T / F
4. Americans went on to a ship in Boston harbour and threw boxes of tea into the sea. T / F
5 The tea on the ships belonged to the British government. T / F
6 After the 'Tea Party', the British government closed Boston harbour. T / F

3 **Helen, a student, is giving a presentation to her class about 'The Boston Tea Party'. Listen and check your answers.**

Mini-project A moment in time

4 **Write a project about an important event in your country's history.**

Look for information on the internet or in a library. Write a text to include:
- A description of what happened.
- Why it is considered so important now.

Use pictures to illustrate the text and present the information as a poster to your class.

UNIT 1   13

UNIT 2 Space and beyond

1 Read the texts.

In this unit

You learn
- past continuous vs past simple
- past perfect
- narrative tenses (Revision)
- words for travel

and then you can
- give reasons
- talk about your journey to school

A When Dennis Tito stepped out of a space shuttle in the early hours of May 6th 2001, he had a big smile on his face. He had just spent nearly seven days in space and had become the world's first space tourist. He had paid $20 million dollars for his trip on the Russian Soyuz rocket. He was not the first non-astronaut in space though. In 1984, the engineering company McDonnell Douglas gave NASA $66,000 to take Charlie Walker, a person who worked for them, on their STS-41D flight to do some research.

B A space shuttle takes 90 minutes to orbit the earth. In these 90 minutes, daylight and night time constantly change for the astronauts. In fact, they see 16 sunsets and 16 sunrises! Altogether, 45 minutes of the journey are spent in daylight, and 45 minutes in the dark.

C Astronauts on the shuttle can choose from about 100 different food items and 50 drinks. However, a word of warning - the taste of food often changes in space and your favourite food on the ground might taste disgusting 200 kilometres above the earth.

D The Russians were the first to travel into space but the Americans were the first to send a man to the moon. When Neil Armstrong took his first steps on the moon, millions were watching him on TV back home. Of course, everyone knows Armstrong was the first man on the moon. But did you know that his Apollo 11 mission left a plaque on the Moon? It says, 'Here men from the planet Earth first set foot upon the Moon July 1969, A.D. We came in peace for all mankind.'

E Space travel has always been a dangerous business. Two of the most tragic accidents in the last 30 years were the Challenger and Columbia space shuttle disasters. In 1986 The Challenger had only been in the sky for a minute when it exploded. In 2003 the Columbia broke up while it was re-entering the earth's atmosphere. On both flights all seven members of the crew died.

2 Match the titles with the correct paragraph from the text. There is one additional title.

1 A 'day' in space? ☐
2 When things go wrong ☐
3 Eating in space ☐
4 A message on the moon ☐
5 Paying passengers ☐
6 Who owns space? ☐

Get talking Giving reasons

3 Listen and repeat.

A Why was Dave so angry?
B Because someone had stolen his wallet.

A Why was Shenna so tired?
B Because she hadn't slept all night.

4 Work with a partner. Look at the pictures and say the moods.

sad   nervous   excited   happy   hungry   bored

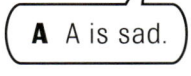
A A is sad.

B B is …

5 Work with a partner. Choose a prompt from below and act out dialogues like the ones in Exercise 3.

A Why was George sad?
B Because his friend had forgotten his birthday.

- watch TV all day
- not study for exam
- friend forget birthday
- get ticket for favourite band
- pass driving test
- not eat all day

UNIT 2   15

Language Focus

Vocabulary Travel

1 Match the sentences and the pictures.

Minnie is a pilot. Every day she flies from London Gatwick to Munich and back.

1 Minnie sets off for work at about 5.30 am.
2 She gets into her car.
3 She gets to the airport at about 6.10 am.
4 She gets on the plane at 6.50 am, half an hour before the passengers.
5 The plane takes off at 7.30 am.
6 The journey takes about an hour and a half. The plane lands at about 9 am.
7 After a rest in Munich she flies back. She gets off the plane at about 4 pm.
8 She drives home. She gets out of the car at about 5 pm.

Get talking Talking about your journey to school

 2 Write the phrases on the right under the questions. Then listen and check.

A How do you get to school?
B 1 ....
A What time do you set off?
B 2 ....

A What time do you get to school?
B 3 ....
A So how long does the journey take?
B 4 ....

> I leave the house at twenty past eight.
>
> I arrive at about ten to nine.
>
> Half an hour
>
> On foot usually but my mum takes me by car if I'm late.

3 Practise the dialogues with a partner. Then find out how your partner gets to school.

16 UNIT 2

Grammar

Past continuous vs past simple

1 **Look at the example and circle the two actions. Which action is the shorter?**

In 2003 the Columbia broke up while it was re-entering the earth's atmosphere.

2 **Look at the pictures and write sentences.**

1 Steve race down the hill / he fall off.

2 Jeff cook / a bird fly into the window.

3 Oliver fish / he see a crocodile.

4 Susan walk on the beach / a wave hit her

5 Julia run to school / the clock strike nine

6 Lana stand at the bus stop / a car soak her with water

Past perfect

3 **Look at the examples and answer the questions.**

A When Dennis Tito had a smile on his face, he had just spent nearly seven days in space.
B In 1986 The Challenger had only been in the sky for a minute, when it exploded.

1 In sentence A, why did Tito have a smile on his face?
2 In sentence B, did The Challenger explode as it took off or after it had taken off?

Rule
We use the Past perfect to emphasise that one action in the past happened before another.

4 **Circle the verb that is in the Past perfect tense.**

1 I hadn't finished my homework but I still went to bed.
2 After she had done the washing up she read her book.
3 When James arrived home he found someone had taken his TV.
4 I didn't buy the coat because I hadn't brought enough money with me.
5 When I got to school I realised I had left my books at home.

5 Complete the sentences using the Past perfect and the Past simple tense.

1. When I .... her face, I knew I .... her before. (see/meet)
2. He .... two pizzas because he .... all day. (order/not eat)
3. I .... so I .... the exam really difficult. (not study/find)
4. Ana .... home because she .... all her money. (go/spend)

Narrative tenses (Revision)

6 Look at the sentences from the text on page 14 and answer the questions.

A He had paid $20 million dollars for his trip.
B McDonnell Douglas gave NASA $66,000 to take Charlie Walker on their flight.
C When Dennis Tito stepped out of a space shuttle he had a big smile on his face.
D Did you know that his Apollo 11 mission left a plaque on the Moon?
E When Neil Armstrong took his first steps on the moon, millions were watching him on TV.

Which sentences contain an example of:

1. the Past simple with a regular verb?   Sentence C
2. the Past simple with an irregular verb?   ....
3. a Past simple question?   ....
4. the Past continuous?   ....
5. the Past perfect?   ....

7 Complete the short story using words from the box.

| got | were walking | had left | didn't take |
| took | had just got in | was shining | were moving |

It was a beautiful morning. The sun ¹............. and there was a cool breeze in the air. It was the perfect day for a picnic. Everyone ²............. into the car. The kids were really excited. A day at the beach and a picnic – the perfect day. The journey there ³............. long and we were soon there. We ⁴............. everything out of the car and started to go down to the beach. While we ⁵............., we saw dark clouds out at sea. They ⁶............. quickly towards us. We ran back to the car, just in time. We ⁷............. when the rain started. Oh well, we still had the picnic. A picnic in the car could be fun. Then Mum opened the picnic basket. I looked at her face and knew immediately. She ⁸............. the picnic at home!

8 Look at the pictures. Choose one to create a story with a partner. Then tell the story to the class. Use the sentences below to start.

As they set off into the jungle, they did not know what was waiting for them …

As the plane took off I realised I'd dropped my passport somewhere …

UNIT 2

Skills

Listening

1 Listen to the radio advert and complete the text.

THE RACE FOR SPACE

Human history is full of stories of explorers who have risked their lives to go places no-one has ever been to before – from the top of the highest mountain, to the bottom of the deepest sea. Would you like to join them? You can win $[1]............... million at the same time!

We offer the Ansari X prize to the first people to build a spaceship that can be used more than once. Interested? These are the rules.

1 The spaceship must be able to carry [2]................ adults.
2 The spaceship must reach a height of [3]............... This height is where a space orbit begins.
3 The spaceship must return with no [4]................ and no injury to any of the crew.
4 A second flight must be made within [5]................ weeks, using the same spacecraft.
5 No government [6].................. can be used in the project.

Does that sound easy? What are you waiting for?

2 Listen to the radio news and tick (✓) the correct options.

1 Which spacecraft won the Ansari prize?

a) Canadian Arrow ☐   b) SpaceShipOne ☐   c) da Vinci Wild Fire ☐

2 How high did the spacecraft fly?
   a) 100km ☐   b) 110km ☐   c) 115km ☐
3 When did the flight take place?
   a) 4/10/2004 ☐   b) 4/11/2004 ☐   c) 14/10/2004 ☐
4 Who flew the plane?
   a) Peter Diamandis ☐   b) Paul Allen ☐   c) Brian Binnie ☐
5 Which company wants to use SpaceShipOne for commercial flights?
   a) Virgin Atlantic ☐   b) Virgin Space ☐   c) Virgin Galactic ☐
6 How much will a flight into space cost?
   a) $20,000 ☐   b) $200,000 ☐   c) $2,000,000 ☐
7 How many people does Richard Branson want to put into space in the next five years?
   a) 3,000 ☐   b) 13,000 ☐   c) 30,000 ☐

UNIT 2   19

Listening

  Listen to the poem and complete the sentences with the correct words.

Journey to Mars

I wish I could go back in [1].........
To a place which I called mine.
Twenty years ago you would find
Life was simple and people were [2].........

But now the streets echo to the [3].........
Of so much trouble all around.
Of people mean and [4].........
Children neglected and needy.

I'm going to Mars
up among the [5].........
I'm leaving this town.
Letting everyone down.
I'm leaving my [6]......... behind.
Out of sight and out of mind.

With a [7]......... and tired face
I travel up into space.
No money for a return flight
On my own, I hope I'm [8].........
A journey into the unknown.
A new world, a new home.

4 Read the poem and decide if the statements are T (True) or F (False).

1 The man is happy because he is going to the moon. T / F
2 He is leaving his family behind. T / F
3 The rocket leaves in a few minutes. T / F
4 He plans to come back soon. T / F

Speaking and writing

5 Discuss the questions with a partner. Then write a story about the poem.

1 Who is this man? (Name, age, profession etc).
2 Who is he leaving behind? Why can't they go with him?
3 Why has he got to leave?
4 Where is he going and why can't he come back?
5 What is going to happen when he arrives at the new world?

6 Read out your stories about the man in the poem.

Check your progress Units 1 and 2

1 Complete the names of the objects.

1 football bo _ _ _
2 a pair of glo _ _ _
3 cycling hel _ _ _
4 swimming go _ _ _ _ _
5 a pair of tra _ _ _ _ _
6 football sho _ _ _

☐ 6

2 Complete the sentences.

1 He sets _ _ _ for work at 7am.
2 I go to school _ _ foot – it's not far.
3 We need to get to the a _ _ _ _ _ _ now to catch the plane.
4 When I get _ _ a plane, I'm really scared.
5 Our plane takes _ _ _ at 9am.
6 Did you have a good j _ _ _ _ _ _ here?
7 The plane l _ _ _ _ at 11am, so we'll take the bus after that.
8 How does your mum _ _ _ to work?
9 How long does it t_ _ _ to get to school?

☐ 8

3 Complete the dialogues.

Sam What ¹............... you doing?
Dave ²............... surfing the Internet. And you?
Sam Not much – I'm really bored.
Dave Why are you so bored?
Sam ³............... I can't think of anything to do.
Dave Why don't you come round? We can do something together.
Sam Great! See you in half an hour.

Shop assistant ⁴............... I help you?
Harry Yes, I need a blue football shirt.
Shop assistant What ⁵............... do you take?
Harry This one looks good. Can I ⁶............... it on, please?
Shop assistant Sure. Go ahead.

☐ 6

4 Write the questions.

1 ....
   Yes, I love tennis!
2 ....
   Emily's training to become an astronaut.
3 ....
   John broke his dad's clock.

☐ 6

5 Complete the sentences with the correct form of the Present continuous.

1 Sam and Dave .... (talk) on the phone.
2 I .... (try) to help you!
3 You .... (not / listen) to me!
4 .... (we / leave) now?
5 We must be quiet – my brothers .... (study)!
6 .... (she / shop) for clothes?

☐ 12

6 Circle the correct tense.

1 I *had finished / have finished* all my homework when he rang.
2 *Have you ever played / Are you ever playing* football for your school?
3 I *don't like / am not liking* many sports but I *am loving / love* swimming.
4 She *is sleeping / sleeps* so don't wake her up.
5 What *are you doing / do you do* on Saturdays?

☐ 6

7 Write the missing words.

Last week I went to a football match at school. It was a great game and I ¹.......... enjoying the action when a player was injured and had to go off. It was bad news for my team because we ².......... losing 2-0 and there ³.......... only half an hour left to play.

Then, the coach came up to me and asked me if I could play! Luckily, I ⁴.......... brought my kit with me. So I quickly changed, pulled my boots on and ran onto the pitch. I ⁵.......... never scored for my team so I don't know why the coach chose me, but I did my best. You're not going to believe this, but I scored three goals! We ⁶.......... the match and the coach said it was all thanks to me!

☐ 6

TOTAL ☐ 50

UNIT 2 21

Trains, planes and automobiles!

1 Read the facts and circle T (True) or F (False). Listen and check your answers.

1 From 1836 to 1926, a man had to walk in front of all cars to warn people that they were coming. T/F
2 In 1962, John Glenn became the first American to circle the Earth in the Friendship 7. T/F
3 There is a building where they build airships which is so tall that clouds form and it rains inside. T/F
4 The woman pilot, Amelia Earhart, set three world records for flying in 1932. T/F
5 In 1939, the Graf Zeppelin airship flew non-stop around the world. T/F

2 Read and complete the text with the numbers in the box below. Compare your answers with a partner.

| 23 | 1901 | 1999 | 1581 | three | 20 million | 2,200 |

Unusual solutions to transport problems – past and present

From tuk-tuks to sky trains in Thailand
Tuk-tuks are ¹............-wheeled vehicles with a place for the driver in the front. People use them for short journeys in the big cities in Thailand. Tuk-tuk engines make a funny sound (that's how it gets its name).
The fastest and cleanest way to travel around Bangkok is by SkyTrain. They built the SkyTrain in ²............ to solve the terrible traffic problem in the city. It originally had ³............ stations but they are building more all the time.

The view from the sky in Germany
It looks very modern, but the monorail, in Wuppertal, Germany opened over 100 years ago in ⁴............ and it's the oldest working monorail in the world. The trains run on electricity and they never stop due to bad weather. Of course, being ten metres above the streets, they never get stuck in traffic either! The monorail carries over ⁵............ passengers a year.

The sedan chair
This is basically just a covered seat on two long pieces of wood. There is a man at the front and another at the back to carry the chair and its passenger. We don't know the exact history of the sedan chair, but we know they existed in the Han Dynasty in China about ⁶............ years ago.

The first sedan chair appeared in England around the year ⁷............, but it was not popular.

3 Now answer the questions.

1 How did the tuk-tuk get its name?
2 How old is the German monorail?
3 In your opinion, which is the best transport?
4 List the advantages and disadvantages of each.

4 **Over 2 U!** World cities are becoming more congested and more polluted. Work in groups. Design a new eco-friendly form of transport.

MORE! And now you can watch *School Reporters!*

UNIT 2

Alien worlds

Emily was a quiet kid. She didn't say much, even to her mother. Her father was always too busy to listen anyway. She never caused any problems. Her grades at school were good. She got on well with everyone, so her mother never worried, until the space paintings.

Emily had always loved to paint and she was good at it, too – very good. She spent all her pocket money on paint and paper. She'd started painting when she was seven. At first it had always been animals, flowers and other things that she saw out of her bedroom window. As she got older, her subjects changed: cars, then people and then sports events. Nothing strange there.

But then one day Emily found something new to paint – scenes of outer space. But these weren't pictures of Mars or Saturn and its rings. These were paintings of weird and wonderful worlds. They showed alien cities on a planet that had three suns. And there were strange forests where strange animals lived. Emily's mother sometimes looked at the paintings, and although she didn't know why, she felt a little bit scared. There was something a bit too real about the scenes. She asked her daughter where her ideas came from.

'They're places I go at night,' she explained.
'What, in your dreams?' she asked.
'Yeah, sort of,' Emily replied.

Emily's mother wanted to talk to her husband about the pictures, but she didn't. Emily's father was a writer. A few years before, he had written a very successful science fiction series for TV. He was famous and got lots of work. But now people were starting to forget about him, because he hadn't come up with anything good for a long time. So he had become depressed. He didn't want to talk to anyone, and he often got angry very quickly if someone disturbed him. Emily was in her room. She had run out of paint, but she had no pocket money left. She couldn't disturb her dad. He was in his office and no-one was allowed to go in there – not even Emily's mother. Emily didn't want to wait, so she picked up some of her paintings and set off for the art shop. She explained to the owner that she needed some paint but she hadn't got any money. She asked the man if he wanted to buy some of her space scenes. He gave her £20 for four of them.

A few days later, Emily's dad was walking past the art shop when he stopped and looked in the window. He saw the four paintings that Emily had done. He was fascinated by them. He walked into the shop and bought them.

Emily's dad took the paintings home and put them on the wall in his office. He sat down in his chair, looked at the paintings and started to write. For the next week, neither Emily nor her mother saw her dad. Day after day, night after night, he locked himself in his office. All they heard was the sound of him working at his computer.

Then one day he came out of the office. They had never seen him so happy.

'It's finished,' he told them. 'My masterpiece.'

A week later they were celebrating. The TV studio had loved his ideas for his new series and they were going to start filming it as soon as possible. A famous Hollywood actor was going to be in it. The series was simply called 'Alien Worlds'.

Read MORE for pleasure

For **MORE!** Go to www.cambridge.org/elt/more and do a quiz on this text.

UNIT 2

UNIT 3 Shopping

In this unit

You learn
- should(n't)/ought(n't)
- gerunds
- words for money and shopping

and then you can
- say what people ought to do
- talk about shopping

1 Listen and read.

Greg Boy, I'm exhausted! Walking round the shops is really tiring!

Emily I know. That's why I like shopping online.

Greg Really? You shouldn't do a lot of online shopping, you know – it can be a bit dangerous.

Emily I don't think so. Well, I've never had a problem anyway. And buying things online is so easy!

Greg That's true – anyway, I can't shop online.

Emily Why not?

Greg I haven't got a debit card.

Emily You ought to have a debit card. They're useful.

Greg Yes, I know. I'm getting one, but it hasn't arrived yet. Actually, it's taking a long time – we asked the bank for it two weeks ago.

Emily I think you should find out what's happening.

Greg Yeah, you're right.

Emily Oh look – there's Asher! Hi, Ash!

Asher Hi you two. Listen, there's a great new CD shop in Station Road – you should go and have a look. They've got a fantastic second-hand section.

Emily Second-hand? No chance! I don't want to buy things that someone else has used.

Asher Oh come on Emily – they're CDs, not clothes!

Emily Well, maybe I'll go, but not now. I ought to go home.

Greg OK – see you, Emily! Now Asher – where's this CD store?

2 Tick (✓) the correct answer.

1 Emily likes
a) shopping online. ☐   b) buying second-hand clothes. ☐
c) walking around shops. ☐

2 Greg can't
a) spend a lot of money. ☐   b) pay in cash. ☐   c) shop online. ☐

3 Emily thinks that Greg should
a) find a credit card. ☐   b) talk to his mother. ☐
c) talk to the bank about his debit card.

4 Asher has found
a) a good shop for CDs. ☐   b) a good clothes shop. ☐   c) an old shop for CDs. ☐

5 Emily is going
a) to buy second-hand clothes. ☐   b) to the CD store. ☐   c) home. ☐

Get talking Saying what people ought to do

3 Listen and repeat.

A I don't feel well.
B You ought to go to the doctor.

A I hate shopping.
B You ought to shop online.

A I haven't got enough money for a new bike.
B You ought to buy a second-hand one.

4 Work with a partner. Make similar dialogues. Use an idea from column A and an idea from column B.

A	B
I need some exercise.	… go to your room and study.
I'm really tired.	… read a book.
I've got a test tomorrow.	… go swimming.
I don't know what to do this afternoon.	… go for a walk.
I'm bored.	… watch a film on DVD.
There's nothing good on television.	… have a rest.

UNIT 3   25

Language Focus

Vocabulary Money and shopping

1 Read the texts. Who do you think is speaking? Match each text with a picture.

A

B **C**

We have to be a bit careful with money at the moment. We're going to need a lot of new things when the baby arrives, so we try to *save* our money. I don't mind not buying things. It's still fun *window shopping*. When we do buy things we always pay by *debit card*.

You have to be careful with money when you're a student. When you've bought all your books, paid the rent and bought some clothes, there's not a lot left. You have to be careful not to *waste* it on silly things. I usually buy a lot of *second-hand* things. It's cheaper. I always pay in *cash*.

Money? Money's no problem. I make loads of it and I *spend* loads of it too. I often go on a *shopping spree*. I always buy the best – *brand new* things. TVs, computers, cars. I always pay by *credit card*. It's easier that way.

2 Find the words in italics in the text and write them in the table below.

Things you can do with money:	Ways of paying for something:	Shopping activities:
1.............. You can 2.............. it 3..............	You can pay by 4.............. in 5.............. by 6..............	go on a 7.............. .... do some 8.............. ....

Adjectives to describe things you buy:
9.. 10..

Get talking Talking about shopping

3 Complete the dialogues. Listen and check.

> Only £1.50   Lots of clothes!   Just some second-hand books.
> I have been on a bit of a spending spree.   In cash.

1 **A** What did you buy?
   B 1..............................
   A How much were they?
   B 2..............................
   A How did you pay?
   B 3..............................

2 **A** Where 've you been?
   B 4..............................
   A What did you buy?
   B 5..............................

4 Work with a partner. Practise the dialogues.

Grammar

Should(n't) / ought(n't)

1 Who says these sentences in the dialogue on page 24? Match the sentences and people.

1 You shouldn't do a lot of online shopping.
2 You ought to have a debit card.
3 You should go and have a look.
4 I ought to go home.

a) Emily to Greg.
b) Emily to Asher and Greg.
c) Asher to Emily and Greg.
d) Greg to Emily.

2 Complete the rule with *should / ought to /* infinitive.

We can use ^{1}............... / *shouldn't* to say what we think is a good idea, and to give advice, They are followed by the ^{2}............... of the verb.
We can also use *ought to* + the infinitive of the verb. The negative of ^{3}............... is not used very often.

3 Match the sentences and responses.

1 My room's in a mess.
2 I'm not feeling very well.
3 I think we've upset Joanna.
4 It's raining hard now.
5 I get really bad marks at school.
6 Bob's had another accident.

a) Perhaps you should work harder.
b) You ought to tidy it up.
c) I don't think we should go out.
d) You ought to see a doctor.
e) He shouldn't drive so fast.
f) Yes, we ought to say 'sorry'.

4 Complete the sentences with the phrases below.

| should go | shouldn't go | should do | ought to buy |
| should ask | should ask | ought to learn | ought to tell |

1 **A** We're lost! **B** You're right. I think we .... someone for directions.
2 **A** I've lost John's pen. **B** Well, I think you .... him.
3 **A** How can I get better grades? **B** I think you .... your homework.
4 **A** I feel terrible. **B** Perhaps you .... to the doctor's.
5 **A** Our TV is really old. **B** You're right. Dad .... a new one.
6 **A** I'm going to Peru on holiday. **B** Great! You .... some Spanish before you go.
7 **A** The teacher gets angry with me sometimes. **B** I don't think you .... so many questions.
8 **A** The sign says 'Do not disturb'. **B** You .... in.

UNIT 3

Gerunds

5 Read the sentences from the dialogue on page 24. Circle the correct verbs.

1 *Walk / Walking* round the shops is really tiring!   2 *Buy / Buying* things online is so easy!

6 Complete the rule. Write *subject* and *–ing*.

The Gerund (the ¹............ form of a verb) can be used as the ²............ or as the object of a verb.

7 Complete the sentences with the verbs below.

watching   doing   playing   eating   going   staying   washing

1 I don't like .... in expensive restaurants.
2 .... online games is really boring!
3 .... examinations is the hardest thing for me.
4 I love .... in nice hotels when we go on holiday.
5 .... the dishes is the worst job in the world!
6 .... to the cinema is OK, but I prefer .... films on TV.

8 Complete the sentences with the gerund of the verb in brackets.

1 .... old films on TV is great fun. (watch)
2 I really don't like .... very much. (dance)
3 .... clothes is my brother's favourite thing. (buy)
4 .... my dog for a walk is good exercise. (take)
5 I hate .... late for school. (be)

9 Complete each sentence using the idea in the picture.

1 Brad really enjoys *listening* to music.
2 .... needs a lot of practice.
3 .... with my friends is my favourite thing.

4 My father loves ....
5 .... is the best thing to do on winter mornings.
6 Jennifer can't stand .... in the rain.

28   UNIT 3

Skills

Reading and speaking

1 Read the quiz and complete it with the words below.

bought   spree   buy   shopping   save   window   by   cash

Is your shopping out of control?

1. Your grandmother gives you €50 for your birthday. Do you:
   [A] go straight to the shopping centre?
   [B] buy a DVD and .... the rest?
   [C] put it all in the bank?

2. Monday is a holiday from school. Do you
   [A] arrange a big shopping spree with your friends?
   [B] go out for the day with your family?
   [C] stay in and do your English assignment?

3. Do you usually pay for something:
   [A] .... credit card?
   [B] by debit card?
   [C] in ....?

4. When was the last time you .... something?
   [A] today
   [B] last week
   [C] last month

5. What do you spend most of your time on the computer doing?
   [A] on-line ....
   [B] playing games
   [C] chatting with friends

6. You walk past your favourite shop. It's closed. Do you:
   [A] spend 10 minutes doing some .... shopping?
   [B] have a quick look in the window and then walk on?
   [C] walk straight past?

7. You need a new computer. Do you:
   [A] .... a brand new one?
   [B] look in the newspaper for a second-hand one?
   [C] see if any of your friends have got a spare one?

2 Discuss the questions with a partner and choose your answers.

3 Look at the key. Work out your score and find out what kind of shopper you are. Do you agree?

Key:
All answer A's = 2 points
All answer B's = 1 point
All answer C's = 0 points

10 – 14 points: You live for the weekend and the chance to get out into the shopping centre. And when the shops aren't open, you're probably online buying things. Do you think it would be a good idea to find another hobby?

5 – 9 points: You enjoy a good day's shopping every now and then but it's not the most important thing in your life. You have your shopping really under control.

0 – 4 points: You really don't enjoy shopping at all, do you? There's just one question; if you don't like shopping, how do you ever get new things? It's time you learned to overcome your fear.

UNIT 3   29

Reading and listening

4 Read the text and find out what the rule of *Buy Nothing Day* is.

What is *Buy Nothing Day*? It's a day where you challenge yourself, your family and friends to stop shopping and enjoy life. Anyone can take part. All you need to do is spend a day without spending!

The message is simple, shop less - live more! The challenge is to try simple living for a day, spend time with family and friends, rather than spend money on them.

Of course, *Buy Nothing Day* isn't about changing your lifestyle for just one day – we want it to be something you think about every day. We want people to make a commitment to buying less, recycling more and challenging companies to clean up and be fair.

To celebrate this year we are holding swap shops, where you can exchange your things with other people, free concerts and shows and, best of all, a cut up your credit card table. Remember, there is only one rule – BUY NOTHING!

5 Listen to Mark Goodwill talking about *Buy Nothing Day* and circle the correct answer.

1 *Buy Nothing Day* is:
  A less than five years old.
  B less than ten years old.
  C more than ten years old.

2 *Buy Nothing Day* is celebrated:
  A in the UK only.
  B in Europe only.
  C all over the world.

3 The organisers think that shopping is:
  A bad for the environment.
  B a waste of money.
  C bad for our health.

4 A shopping free zone is an area:
  A where you don't pay for anything.
  B where shopping is banned.
  C people do things to get shoppers' attention.

5 To organise a 'choo-choo' you need
  A 13 people.
  B 15 people
  C 20 people

6 One thing you should do is
  A give out leaflets.
  B annoy people who are shopping.
  C have fun.

Reading

6 Read the extracts from the emails and answer the questions.

1 How much pocket money does Sam get?
2 How much was the CD that Ollie bought?
3 How old is Donna's dad?
4 What is the name of the person in the picture?

...I bought a CD on Saturday. I gave the guy a £10 note and he gave me change. However, when I got home I checked my change and I realised that he'd given me change for £50. That means I got the CD and I'm £42 richer. That means I can get the new James Bond game and still have some money left. The thing is I feel a bit bad about keeping it. It's a lot of money and the guy who served me will probably have to pay out of his wages. But then £42 is a lot of money. It could make me very happy... (Ollie)

...It's my dad's birthday on Sunday and I want to get him a really special present, something to say thanks for the help he's given me with my exams. Plus it's his last year in the forties! The only problem is I don't know what to get him. He loves old books on fishing but I've no idea where I could find them. So I'm thinking of something else. He's on a diet so no chocolate. He doesn't really like clothes. I don't know. He's so difficult. I don't suppose you've got any ideas. I mean, what would you buy your dad?... (Donna)

... I was in Top Girl on Saturday. You'll never guess what – they've got some really cool leather boots. They're beautiful. I was going to buy them and then I looked at the price £99.99. That's nearly £100. I haven't got that sort of money. I've only got £50. It would take me another two months' pocket money to have enough (and that's if I don't spend a penny on anything else). But I so want them. They'd be perfect for Molly's birthday next month. Oh what am I going to do? ... (Sam)

Speaking and writing

7 Work in small groups. Discuss what you think Sam, Ollie and Donna should do.

8 Choose one of the emails and write a reply saying what you think the person should do.

Sounds right Spelling

9 Practise spelling out loud the names of the people who wrote the emails in Exercise 6. Then think of five people in your class and spell their names to your partner who writes them down. Then change roles.

UNIT 3   31

Space travel

Key words

jet of water	mass	force	reaction engine
orbit	orbiter	accelerate	rocket booster
hose	launch	thrust	mph (miles per hour)

1 Read the text and write three questions to ask your partner.

How things work – rocket engines

How do rockets work? Here are a few of the problems that space engineers have to solve when they build rockets:
- What kind of engine can get a rocket into space?
- How will the rocket cope with extreme temperatures? – metal gets very hot at high speeds.
- How can they get the rocket back into the earth's atmosphere?

Today – the engine

Car engines use the principle of rotation to turn the wheels. Rockets don't have wheels, so a different kind of engine is needed; an engine that can 'throw' the rocket (a huge and heavy piece of metal) hundreds of kilometres into the sky.

What a rocket needs is a reaction engine. Reaction engines work on a famous scientific principle, discovered by Sir Isaac Newton. The principle says: 'For every action, there is an equal and opposite reaction.'

Let's look at this principle more simply. Have you ever seen firefighters dealing with a fire using a big water hose? These hoses throw out a weight of water that produces a force in the opposite direction. This force can be quite strong and this is why there are usually two firefighters holding the hose. If the jet of water was too strong for the firefighters, they would go flying back in the opposite direction.

A rocket engine is generally throwing mass in the form of a high-pressure gas. The engine throws the mass of gas out in one direction in order to get a reaction in the opposite direction. The mass comes from the weight of the fuel that the rocket engine burns. The burning process accelerates the mass of fuel so that it comes out of the rocket at high speed.

If you have ever seen the Space Shuttle launch, you will know that there are three parts:
- The Orbiter
- The big external tank
- The two solid rocket boosters (SRBs)

The Orbiter weighs 165,000 pounds empty. The external tank weighs 78,100 pounds empty. The two solid rocket boosters weigh 185,000 pounds empty each. But then you have to load in the fuel. Each SRB holds 1.1 million pounds of fuel. The external tank holds 143,000 gallons of liquid oxygen (1,359,000 pounds) and 383,000 gallons of liquid hydrogen (226,000 pounds). The whole vehicle – shuttle, external tank, solid rocket boosters and all the fuel – has a total weight of 4.4 million pounds at launch. 4.4 million pounds to get 165,000 pounds in orbit! All of that fuel is being thrown out the back of the Space Shuttle at a speed of perhaps 6,000 mph. The SRBs burn for about two minutes and generate about 3.3 million pounds of thrust each at launch. The three main engines burn for about eight minutes, generating 375,000 pounds of thrust each during the burn.

Mini-project Finding out about space

2

Choose one of the following questions. Go to a library or use the internet to find out more about it. Write a short text. Add images if you can.

- One of the challenges with space travel is how to get a spacecraft safely back to earth. Why is this so? How can scientists make sure that a rocket doesn't burn up under the high temperatures?
- The United States and Russia have had orbiting space stations since 1971 and are now cooperating with other nations to build the International Space Station, a place that will make it possible for humans to stay in space permanently. What will the space station look like? What will it be like to live and work in space? What problems are involved in establishing a space station? What will it be used for?
- Apophis, a 45-million-ton rock, a so-called asteroid, is orbiting the sun at 28,000 mph. If it hits Earth, it could easily destroy a large city. In 2029, it'll be closer to us than our moon is. Find out more about asteroids. What are they? What does modern science say could be done to avoid an asteroid's collision with planet Earth?

UNIT 3   33

UNIT 4 A working life

 1 Listen and read.

In this unit

You learn
- *be going to* / Present continuous (Revision)
- future time clauses
- adjectives for personality

and then you can
- say what you want to do
- talk about personality and jobs

What do you want to do when you leave school?

I want to be a soldier. So as soon as I leave school, I'll join the army. My mum's not so happy about that. But I'd love to be part of a UN peace-keeping force. There are lots of people in the world who need protection. I'd like to help them.

I'm going to be a dancer. I know it's a bit unusual for a boy and a couple of my friends make jokes about it. But it's what I love – there's nothing I like more. My mum and dad are cool about it. They know I'm good at dancing and they know I'm hard-working, too.

Are you doing anything now to help you get where you want to be?

You have to be fit to get into the army so I work out a lot. And in about 6 months' time, I'm having my first interview with the army to see about joining, so I'm getting ready for that.

Yes, of course. I have lessons every week, and next summer, I'm taking a course in Flamenco dancing in Madrid. After I finish it, I'll be a much better dancer.

What jobs would you never want to do?

I could never do anything that involves working with children. I could never be a teacher, for example. I'm not patient enough. I'd hate to teach someone like me, for example!

I don't think I could be a doctor or a dentist. I don't like the sight of blood. It's funny because my dad's a dentist and my mum's a nurse.

What's more important – money or enjoying what you do?

Money is important. I mean, you can't live without it. But I don't need a lot of money to be happy. I think it's more important to enjoy what you do – so no matter what I do, I'm going to enjoy every minute.

Both are important. Most dancers don't get paid much money, but I'm going to make a lot of money, I think. Because I know I'm going to be successful. Am I arrogant? Maybe. Ambitious? Absolutely!

34 UNIT 4

2 Write *Mandy* or *Philip* in each space.

1 .... wants to be a soldier.
2 ....'s parents think he/she is making a good choice.
3 .... wants to help people.
4 .... wants to do something he/she is very good at.
5 ....'s parents work in healthcare.
6 .... wouldn't like to work with young people.
7 .... wants to make a lot of money.
8 .... doesn't care a lot about money.

Get talking Saying what you want to do.

3 Match the questions with the possible answers. There are two answers for each question. Then listen and check.

1 What are you going to do when you leave school?
2 Why did you choose that?
3 What job would you never want to do?
4 Why?

a) I'd hate to be a farmer.
b) I want to be a policeman.
c) Because I love animals.
d) I could never be a writer.
e) Because I don't like working alone.
f) I'm not sure yet, but maybe a vet.
g) Because I like helping people.
h) Because I don't like getting up very early.

4 Work with a partner. Ask them the questions from Exercise 3 then change over.

A What are you going to do when you leave school?

B I'm not sure yet, perhaps I'll be a teacher.

Language Focus

Vocabulary Personality adjectives

  1 Complete the sentences with the correct word. Use their names to help you. Then listen and check.

ambitious
hard-working
creative
helpful
easy-going
patient
~~friendly~~
polite

1 Freda is *friendly*

2 Alan is ....

3 Hannah is ....

4 Eric is ....

5 Harry is ....

6 Patricia is ....

7 Chris is ....

8 Polly is ....

 2 Match the beginnings and endings of the sentences. Then listen and check.

1 Ernie does things quickly and always really well –
2 Ian has lots of ideas –
3 Keira always has something nice to say –
4 Irene doesn't need other people to help her –
5 Holly always tells the truth –
6 Ralph does the things he's got to do –

a) she's very independent.
b) she's very honest.
c) he's very imaginative.
d) he's really efficient
e) he's really responsible.
f) she's very kind.

Get talking Talking about personality and jobs

3 Work with a partner. Talk about the jobs on the right. Use the adjectives from Exercise 1. Say what you think.

teacher
doctor
waiter
salesperson
police officer
web designer
nurse
writer

A   I think a police officer needs to be honest.

B   I agree. And responsible, too. What about a teacher?

Grammar

Talking about the future
be going to / Present continuous (Revision)

1 Here are four sentences from the text on page 34. Which sentences:
a talk about someone's intentions? b talk about fixed arrangements for the future?

1 **I'm going to be** a dancer.
2 **I'm going to enjoy** every minute.
3 Next summer **I'm taking** a course in Flamenco dancing.
4 **I'm going to make** a lot of money.

2 Match the sentences with the pictures.

1 He's going to play football. ☐
2 He's playing football on Monday. ☐
3 She's going to have lunch. ☐
4 She's having lunch with Jimmy tomorrow. ☐

OK, Jimmy. See you 12.30 tomorrow for lunch.

3 Write sentences.

1 John / do / homework
John's going to do his homework.

2 Sandra / watch / DVD
....

3 They / wash / dog
....

4 We / have / picnic
....

5 My sister / be / ballet dancer
....

6 He / join / army.
....

4 Choose some things to do tonight and at the weekend. Write them down.
Work with a partner. Ask and answer questions.

Are you going to a disco on Sunday?

No, I'm not. I'm staying at home. What about you?

UNIT 4   37

Future time clauses

5 Match the beginnings and endings of the sentences.

A	B
1 As soon as I leave school,	a) I'll be a better dancer.
2 When I join the army,	b) I'll help to protect people.
3 After I finish the Flamenco course,	c) I'll visit foreign countries.

6 Look at the phrases in column A in Exercise 5. Circle the correct words below to complete the sentences.

1 The phrases talk about actions in *the present / the future*.
2 In the phrases, the verb is in the *present / future* tense.

7 Match the beginnings and endings of the sentences.

1 Please switch the lights off before
2 I'll tell her as soon as
3 I'll leave school when
4 I'll do my homework as soon as
5 He wants to join the army after
6 We'll talk about it when

a) she gets here.
b) the programme finishes.
c) you go home.
d) he leaves school.
e) I get home.
f) I'm sixteen.

8 Circle the correct word and complete the text.

When I ¹(leave)/ will leave school, I think I ² *go / will go* to Canada for a while. Why? Well, I ³ *want / will want* to see the world a bit before I ⁴ *start / will start* work. I think I ⁵ *go / will go* to Toronto. My friend told me that if I ⁶ *stay / will stay* in small hotels and camp sites, it ⁷ *isn't / won't be* very expensive. Well, I'm not so sure! But I ⁸ *check / will check* things out before I ⁹ *go / will go*. But I know I'm going – and as soon as I ¹⁰ *arrive / will arrive* in Canada, I ¹¹ *go / will go* straight to Niagara Falls – that's always been my dream!

9 Complete with *will ('ll)* and the verb at the end of the sentence.

1 I ..'ll.... phone you as soon as I ..get.. my exam results. (phone / get)
2 I don't think it .... before we .... home. (rain / get)
3 I .... round to your place when I .... my homework. (come / finish)
4 As soon as I .... school, I .... a job in a bank. (leave / get)
5 When my parents .... on holiday next week, I .... the house to myself. (go / have)
6 I .... you the money back when my parents .... me my pocket money. (pay / give)

38 UNIT 4

Skills

Reading

1 Read the magazine article and find the answers to these questions.

1 How many hours a day does Lena work?
2 How many days a week does she work?

A Day in the Life of ...

Hi, my name's Lena Diekmann. I'm 19 and I'm from Berlin in Germany. I'm a waitress in the Tea Rooms in the centre of York. I really like my job because no two days are ever the same. My colleagues are great and so is my boss. Anyway, this is my day.

Mornings

I don't start work until 10 o'clock so I usually wake up at about 9. This is great for me because I hate getting up too early. I have breakfast, tea and toast with Marmite (I'm very British!) and walk to work. My flat's not far so it only takes me about 10 minutes.

When I get to work I put on my uniform and start work. I like waiting tables. It's a great way of meeting people and I've already made a lot of friends working here. I love talking to the customers, but sometimes I have to be quite patient with them.

You love it or you hate it. I love it!

Afternoons

I finish my morning shift at 2.30pm after the lunchtime rush. I have two hours before I have to start again. Three times a week I have English lessons (the other days I go home for a quick nap). One of the reasons I'm here is to learn English. My job is a great way of practising it but I still need to learn as well. My afternoon shift is from 4.30 to 7pm. It usually flies by – it's 7 o'clock before I know it!

Evenings

I love the evenings. Time to spend some of the money I earn! The job's not very well-paid but the tips are usually good. I usually go out either to the cinema or meet up with friends. At the weekend I usually go clubbing but I have to work on Saturdays and Sundays so I can't stay out too late. If I've got any money left after the weekend, then I go shopping on Tuesdays. It's my only day off.

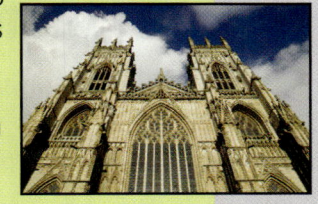

My uniform!

Don't forget to tip the waitress.

York! What a city!

2 Read the article again and decide if the sentences are T (True) or F (False).

1 Lena thinks her job is a bit boring sometimes. T / F
2 She likes all the people she works with. T / F
3 Lena lives close to the restaurant. T / F
4 Lena sometimes needs to be patient. T / F
5 Lena has English lessons every day. T / F
6 Lena says her afternoon shift passes very quickly. T / F
7 She doesn't earn a lot of money in the job. T / F
8 Lena works at the weekend. T / F

Listening

3 **Listen to Kelly and then Liam talking about their job interviews. Answer the questions.**

Who:
1. had a good interview?
2. took a dog to the interview?
3. wants to work for a newspaper?
4. has worked as a shop assistant?
5. wants to be a receptionist?
6. wants to start working very soon?
7. said they like working with people?
8. works for the school newspaper?

4 **Listen again and match the questions to the answers.**

1. Who is Rover?
2. Why did Kelly take a dog to the interview?
3. What did the interviewer think about the dog?
4. What was Kelly's best answer?
5. Why is Liam happy?
6. What question did the interviewer ask Liam?
7. When did Liam say he could start work?
8. What is Liam waiting for?

a) On Monday.
b) A phone call.
c) Kelly's dog.
d) Your company has an excellent reputation.
e) He didn't seem very happy.
f) Because he had a good interview.
g) Because she had to take him to the vet before.
h) Have you ever worked for a newspaper?

Writing

5 **Complete the text with the words on the left.**

get down
window
wanted
ladder
outdoors
job

My brother is a window cleaner. He likes his ¹................ . He likes working ²................ and he loves talking to people. Yesterday he was cleaning a ³................ when an old woman next door called him. Her cat had climbed a tree and couldn't ⁴................ . He got his ⁵................ and climbed up and got the cat. The woman was very happy and ⁶................ to give my brother some money. Of course my brother didn't take it.

6 **Think of someone in your family. Write a short text about their job.**

40 UNIT 4

Check your progress Units 3 and 4

1 Complete the sentences.

1 We sometimes go w_ _ _ _ _ shopping when we haven't got any money.
2 You shouldn't w_ _ _ _ your money on things you don't need.
3 I bought a s_ _ _ _ _ _-_ _ _ _ computer because the new ones were too expensive.
4 He won a lot of money and went on a shopping s_ _ _ _.
5 He broke my b_ _ _ _ new laptop!
6 Ian always pays by c_ _ _ _ _ card.   ☐ 6

2 Read the descriptions and complete the sentences.

1 She can make amazing things.
   She's c_ _ _ _ _ _ _ _.
2 He wants to succeed in life.
   He's a_ _ _ _ _ _ _ _ _.
3 John's really relaxed – nothing bothers him!
   He's e_ _ _-_ _ _ _ _.
4 Anna is always busy – she never stops.
   She's h_ _ _-_ _ _ _ _ _ _.
5 Tony doesn't mind waiting for things.
   He's very p_ _ _ _ _ _.
6 Barbara always says *please* and *thank you*.
   She's very p_ _ _ _ _.   ☐ 6

3 Complete the dialogues. Use the Present continuous.

A I'm ¹............ (see) my cousin today.
B What time?
A Well, the train is ²............ (arrive) at 3 pm.
B ³............ (meet) him at the station?
A Yes, I ⁴............ (take) a taxi.
B ⁵............ (he/come) alone?
A No, my aunt ⁶............ (come) with him too. We ⁷............ (have) lunch at *The Cedars* tomorrow. Would you like to come?
B No, I'm sorry, I ⁸............ (do) my homework!   ☐ 8

4 Complete the sentences with the correct verb or word for the future time clause.

1 As .... as he ....(arrive), we'll go.
2 She .... (leave) school .... she is 18.
3 We will go swimming ....we .... (finish) work.   ☐ 6

5 Give advice in the following situations.

1 I have to pay a big credit card bill. (not / use / credit card) You ....
2 I want to become a doctor. (study hard) You ....
3 My English friend is going to live in Italy. (learn / Italian) She ....
4 I have to get up early for work tomorrow. (go / bed) You ....
5 My brother isn't feeling well. (see / doctor) He ....   ☐ 10

6 Complete the sentences with the gerund or infinitive of the verbs in brackets.

1 I don't like .... alone. (be)
2 There's nothing I love more than .... in the rain. (walk)
3 Gill's keen on .... (skate)
4 I'm going .... a film tonight. (see)
5 I want .... a job that involves travelling. (do)
6 Is .... too much cream bad for you? (eat)
7 I think you ought .... sorry. (say)
8 Emma hates .... for buses. (wait)   ☐ 8

7 Circle the correct answer.

1 *I am going to be / am being* a pilot.
2 Mum – *I'm going / I will go* out tonight. Is that all right?
3 You spent all your money? How are you *buying / going to buy* food for tomorrow?
4 Try to come to my party – everyone is *going to be / is being* there.
5 Read this book – *you're going to like it / you're liking it*.
6 I think you ought to *say / saying* sorry.   ☐ 6

TOTAL ☐ 50

My progress so far is ...

☺ brilliant! ☐   😐 quite good. ☐   ☹ not great. ☐

UNIT 4 41

Learn MORE about Culture

Beefeaters!

1 Read about the job of a Beefeater.

Do YOU know?
The Yeoman Warders in London are called *Beefeaters*. This is probably because a long time ago, as the bodyguards of the King, they were allowed to eat as much beef as they wanted.

Beefeaters at the Tower of London
There are about 36 Beefeaters at the Tower of London. Work on the tower started in 1060 and the Beefeaters are part of a tradition that goes back 700 years. Many people think that the tower is haunted by ghosts. Some say they have seen the ghosts of people who used to be in prison there. There is a legend that says six ravens (black birds) must be at the tower at all times or the tower will fall down. One Beefeater looks after these birds as his full-time job.

Duties and responsibilities
Officially, the job of the Beefeaters is to look after prisoners in the tower, but they spend most of their time talking to tourists, since there are no longer any prisoners there. Every evening at 10 pm, they take part in the Ceremony of the Keys — when the tower is locked up for the night to protect the Crown Jewels. Beefeaters have to make sure that no one is locked in! Other duties include doing fire and safety checks to make sure everything is under control.

Qualifications
Yeoman Warders must have been in the British Army, Royal Air Force, Royal Marines or Royal Navy for about 20 years. They must have a good record during this time.

Personality
You must enjoy talking to people and answering their questions (and you need to learn the history of the tower so you know the answers!) You need to be polite and easy-going with the visitors — but you also have to be able to control 300 people so that they do as you say and they are not in any danger. In addition, you need to be hard-working — it's a long day sometimes.

Rewards
The warders and their families get a reasonable salary and a small house at the tower which they keep until they retire.

2 Derrick is talking more about his job. Listen and circle the correct answer.

1 You have to spend at least 22 years in the navy, army or air force to become a Beefeater. T / F
2 Derrick has been a Beefeater for 39 years. T / F
3 Derrick wanted the job of Ravenmaster because he gets on well with people. T / F
4 Derrick is going to retire in four years time. T / F
5 The birds are very clever. One of them can speak. T / F

3 Have you got a part-time job? Do you know anyone with an unusual or special job? Tell the class.

4 **Over 2 U!** Who guards the important buildings in your country? Find out about their job, or another job, and write a description. Use Exercise 1 to help you.

MORE! And now you can watch *School Reporters!*

Omelettes and hard work: A recipe for success

On his first day in the UK, in 1990, George Wannous lost all his money. George had left Syria, his country, because a friend who had moved from Syria to Inverness, Scotland, invited him to come to the UK and work on a fruit farm. But George never got to Scotland.

When the 19 year-old Syrian landed at Gatwick airport, he took a train to Victoria station in London, to catch a coach to Scotland. When he got off the train a man approached him and took out a knife. He pointed it at George. 'The man took all my money, everything I had,' George says. 'It was awful.'

George called the London police and two kind police officers felt sorry for him. They gave him some money and put him on a train to Scotland.

For some reason, George got off the train in Manchester and the next day he started to look for a job. First he went to work at a bakery, but at the same time he took other jobs, too. He worked very hard. For half a year, he sold bread in the morning, and in the afternoon he cleaned offices for £3 an hour. For some time he also worked as a taxi driver at night. In 1993, he got a job as a dishwasher at a small café. The manager of the café liked George. He told him to study the menu carefully so he could become a waiter. 'All the food on the menu was new to me,' George says. 'A medium-rare beef burger! In my country we cook everything well done.' George became a waiter, but he slowly worked his way up, and half a year later he became the manager of the café.

When the owner decided to sell the café, George went to the bank to borrow money to buy it. He started to work extremely hard – up to twenty hours a day! When he was tired, he slept in his car in the car park.

That was eleven years ago. George has become successful. He is very clever. Instead of making three-egg omelettes as the old company did, he uses four eggs. George says. 'My friends told me I would lose money selling bigger omelettes for the same price. But I didn't lose money – I got happier customers, and more customers.'

George is 39 now. He's happily married and he's got three children. He has a much bigger café now, and there are eight people working for him. George has made it – thanks to his hard work!

For **MORE!** Go to www.cambridge.org/elt/more and do a quiz on this text.

UNIT 5 Bookworms

In this unit

You learn
- so / such
- phrasal verbs
- words for types of books

and then you can
- give reasons
- talk about books

1 Listen and read.

Asher Hey Emily, I'm really bored. Let's go and hang out at the youth club.
Emily Can't you see I'm reading a book?
Asher Come on. You can finish it later.
Emily I'm sorry. It's such a good book I can't put it down.
Asher What are you reading anyway?
Emily It's a book by Scott Westerfield. It's called *Uglies*.
Asher *Uglies*. What's that about then?
Emily Do you really want to know? Or are you just bored?
Asher How can you say such a thing. Of course, I'm interested. Honestly.
Emily Well, OK. So it all takes place in the future. All kids are Uglies until they're 16. Then they have an operation and turn into Pretties. Pretties are good-looking and mess around and have parties all the time.
Asher It sounds like fun.
Emily Yeah, but it's not what it seems. There's this rebel group of kids who run away to escape the operation. It's called The Smoke. The government are after them before they find out the truth. It's all very exciting.
Asher It all seems very confusing to me.
Emily Yeah, but if you start reading it you'll really get into it, I promise.
Asher You know, I'm so bored I might just do that. Hand over the book.
Emily No way. You'll have to hang on until I finish!

44 UNIT 5

2 Match the sentence halves to make a summary of the dialogue.

1 Asher wants
2 Emily is happy
3 *Uglies* is
4 Pretties are
5 Asher thinks
6 Emily suggests
7 Asher tries to

a) reading her book.
b) what Uglies become after an operation.
c) take the book from Emily.
d) Asher should read the book.
e) about teenage life in the future.
f) the book sounds confusing.
g) to do something.

Get talking Giving reasons

3 Write the answers under the questions. Listen and check.

1 It was so great I didn't want it to end.
2 It was so exciting I couldn't put it down.
3 It was so noisy I couldn't talk to anyone.
4 It was so long I slept most of the way.

A How was the book?
....

B How was the journey?
....

C How was your holiday?
....

D How was the party?
....

4 Work with a partner. Student A chooses a picture to ask about. Student B chooses prompts from the A and B boxes to reply.

A How was the film?
B It was so boring that I walked out of the cinema.

film

rollercoaster

pizza

test

beach

hotel bed

A	B
boring	walk out of cinema
comfortable	get a headache
exciting	want another piece
hot	not want to get out of it
delicious	have another go immediately
difficult	spend all the time in the water

UNIT 5   45

Language Focus

Vocabulary Types of books

1 Match the types of books with the titles.

1 a detective novel
2 a biography
3 poetry
4 short stories
5 non-fiction
6 a book about animals
7 a graphic novel
8 a romance

a) *The Collected Poems of Byron.*
b) *Love in the Spring*
c) *Tears of a Clown and other stories*
d) *Ordinary Genius – the story of Albert Einstein*
e) *Looking after your horse*
f) *How to Write Better*
g) *The Body in the Library*
h) *Batman Returns*

Get talking Talking about books

2 Put the lines in order to make two dialogues. Listen and check.

1 A ☐ So what do you like?
  A ☐ Do you like poetry?
  B ☐ It's OK but it's not my favourite.
  B ☐ Well I quite like short stories but I love graphic novels.

2 C ☐ So what do you like books about?
  C ☐ Do you like books about horses?
  D ☐ Horses? No, I don't.
  D ☐ Football and cars.

3 Work with a partner. Say what you think about the types of books in Exercise 1.

4 Look at the books. What kind of book do you think each one is?

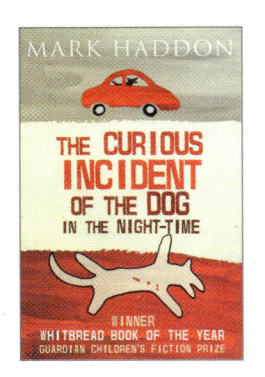

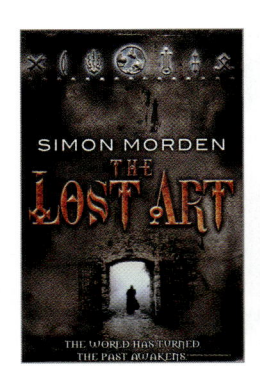

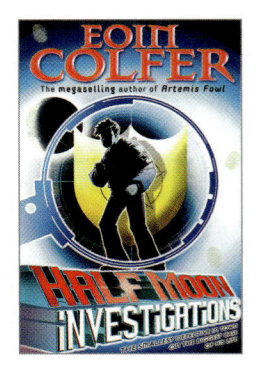

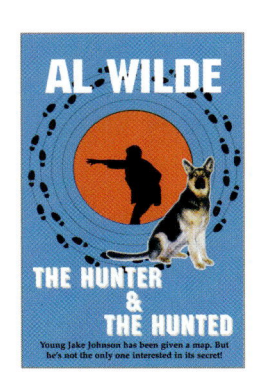

5 Which of these books looks interesting to you? If you had to pick one, which one would it be and why?

I'd pick … because it looks interesting / funny / thrilling / exciting…
I'd pick it, because I like thrillers, love / horror / sci-fi (etc.) stories…
I'd pick it because I've already read … by the same author.

Grammar

So / such

1 **Look at the examples and complete the rule.**

*It's **such** a good book (that) I can't put it down.*
*I'm **so** bored (that) I might just do that.*

Rule
We can use ¹.......... before a noun and ².......... before an adjective to emphasise the quality of the noun or adjective. We can also talk about the result by adding *that* followed by a clause.

2 **Match the pictures and the sentences.**

1. It was such a hot day that we went swimming.
2. I was so bored that I watched TV all day.
3. It was so hot that I burned my mouth.
4. I was feeling so energetic that I went for a swim.
5. I was so thirsty that I drank the whole glass in one go.
6. It was such a scary film that I couldn't watch.
7. The sun was so bright that I had to wear sunglasses.
8. I've got such bad eyesight that I have to wear glasses.

3 **Circle the correct word.**

1. The film was *such/so* long that I fell asleep.
2. I had *such/so* a bad dream that I couldn't back to sleep.
3. The accident was *such/so* serious that they called a helicopter ambulance.
4. The sea was *such/so* dirty that we didn't go in it.
5. I've got *such/so* a bad headache that I'm going to bed.
6. That's *such/so* a great idea, I just might do it.

4 **Rewrite the two sentences to make one. Use the word in brackets.**

1. I was really hungry. I ordered another sandwich. (so)
   I was so hungry that I ordered another sandwich.
2. The test was really difficult. I didn't pass it. (such) ....
3. The computer was very expensive. I couldn't afford it. (so) ....
4. The view was really beautiful. I had to take a photo. (such) ....
5. He speaks really fast. I don't understand a word he says. (so) ....
6. The game was really good. I didn't want it to end. (such) ....

UNIT 5   47

Phrasal verbs

5 Look at the dialogue on page 44 and complete the sentences.

Let's go and ¹............ .... at the youth club.
Then they have an operation and ²............ .... Pretties
Pretties ³............ .... and have parties all the time.
The government are after them before they ⁴............ .... the truth.
If you start reading it you'll really ⁵............ .... it, I promise
You'll have to ⁶............ .... until I finish!

6 Match the phrasal verbs in Exercise 5 with these definitions.

1 become ....
2 discover ....
3 start to enjoy a lot ....
4 have fun ....
5 spend some time ....
6 wait ....

7 The following contain verbs with prepositions. How are they different from phrasal verbs?

There's this rebel group of kids who *run away* to escape the operation.
It's such a good book I can't *put it down*.

Many verbs in English are followed by prepositions. Sometimes this verb-preposition structure can't be immediately understood by looking at the individual words. These are called phrasal verbs.

8 Circle the phrasal verbs in the sentences below. What do they mean?

1 He really takes after his father. They like all the same things.
2 I'm sorry. I've just knocked over your glass of water.
3 Paul, stand up and come here, please.
4 Guess who I ran into today in town. Josh, I haven't seen him for years.
5 Can you turn up the volume? I can't hear a thing.
6 I've taken up judo. I'm not very good yet, but it's just the beginning.

9 Complete the sentences with the phrasal verbs on this page.

1 She really .... her mother.
2 It's a great game. You'll really .... it.
3 Kiss me and I'll .... a prince, I promise.
4 You'll have to .... for a while. The fire service are coming.
5 He's just .... yoga and he's still got a lot to learn.
6 It was really nice to .... you. I haven't seen you for a long time.

48 UNIT 5

Skills

Reading

1 Read the book review. Does Brenda like the book?

Hi, this is Brenda's Books online, and this week the book I'm recommending is one I've been waiting to read for ages. It is, of course, the latest Alex Rider adventure by Anthony Horowitz — *Snakehead*. I've been a big fan of this teenage spy ever since the first novel *Stormbreaker*. This is the seventh book in the series and they just keep getting better.

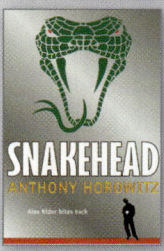

For any of those who have never read an Alex Rider novel (Can there really be anyone out there who's never read an Alex Rider novel?), Horowitz's hero is a kind of junior James Bond who works for MI6 only he's much cooler than James Bond and his missions are more dangerous. In *Snakehead* Alex is in Australia working for the ASS (the Australian Secret Service) in their fight against the Snakehead, a dangerous gang of criminals from South-East Asia. This time Alex has a partner called Ash who used to work with Alex's father. Ash knows secrets from Alex's past and soon Alex is not sure who he can trust any more. The book also features the return of an old enemy whose plans will cause chaos around the world if he is not stopped. Can Alex sort out his problems and save the world? Well I know the answer because I've read the book but I'm not telling you. All I can promise is that you won't be disappointed. It's fast and exciting with action on every page. It's impossible to put down. I read it in two goes and that's only because my mum insisted that I had dinner with the family.

In his introduction Horowitz says 'It's been two years since I wrote my last Alex Rider story. I hope you'll agree it's been worth the wait." It most definitely has.

★★★★

2 Circle T (True) or F (False) for the sentences below.

1 Brenda was already a fan of the Alex Rider books. T / F
2 There have been four books between Stormbreaker and Snakehead. T / F
3 Brenda thinks Snakehead is the best of the Alex Rider books. T / F
4 Alex Rider works with James Bond. T / F
5 Ash is a relative of Alex. T / F
6 Brenda didn't finish the book in one go. T / F
7 Brenda is a bit disappointed that Horowitz took a long time to finish the book. T / F

Listening

3 Listen to Julie, Fred and Farid talking about what they think of reading and about their favourite books. Answer the questions with their names.

Who...
1 prefers TV to books?
2 loves reading
3 is reading a book about a film?
4 likes horror stories?
5 reads two or three books every month?
6 likes fantasy stories
7 likes books for teenage girls?

UNIT 5

Speaking and listening

4 Read the beginning of *Snakehead*. Which of the pictures does it describe?

A   B   C

Splash down.

Alex Rider would never forget the moment of impact, the first shock as the parachute opened and the second – more jolting still – as the module that had carried him back from outer space crashed into the sea. Was it his imagination or was there steam rising up all around him? Maybe it was sea spray. It didn't matter. He was back. That was all he cared about. He had made it. He was still alive.

He was lying on his back, crammed into the tiny capsule with his knees tucked into his chest. Half closing his eyes, Alex experienced a moment of extraordinary stillness. He was motionless. His fists were clenched. He wasn't breathing. Already he found it impossible to believe that the events that had led to his journey into space had really taken place. He tried to imagine himself hurtling around the earth at seventeen and a half thousand miles an hour. It couldn't have happened. It had surely all been part of some incredible dream.

5 Find these words in the text and circle the best definition for each one.

1 jolting:
   a) moving in a sudden strong way   b) quiet   c) in a relaxed way
2 module
   a) a parachute   b) part of a space ship   c) a small boat
3 crammed
   a) with not much room   b) with a lot of room   c) asleep
4 clenched fist
   a) 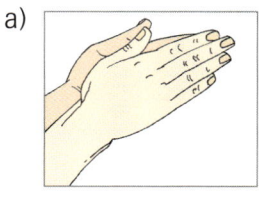   b) 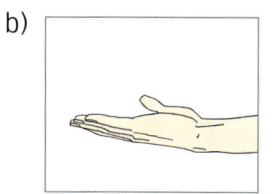   c) 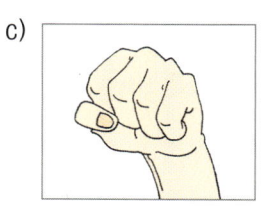
5 hurtling
   a) moving slowly   b) moving quickly   c) moving really quickly

6 "Already he found it impossible to believe that the events that had led to his journey into space had really taken place."

Work with a partner. Decide what those events were. Make up a short story. Tell your story to the rest of the class and vote on the best one.

50 UNIT 5

Speaking and writing

7 **Think of the last book you read and write notes to answer the questions.**

- Title / author?
- What kind of book is it?
- What's it about?
- Did you like it? Why/why not?

8 **Work with a partner. Ask and answer questions about your books.**

9 **Read the review below and answer the questions.**

1. What happens in the book?
2. Did Anahita like it? (Why/why not?)

- Book: Dead Girls Don't Write Letters
- Author: Gail Giles
- What's it about?

Sunny's sister Jazz (who is NOT a nice girl) dies in a fire. Her parents are really sad, but one day Sunny gets a letter from Jazz. 'I'll be coming home soon,' it says. And in fact, one day Jazz turns up. She has turned into a nice, friendly girl, and she knows everything about the family's past. But Sunny asks herself a big question: Who is this stranger who says she's Jazz? She knows that dead girls can't write letters!

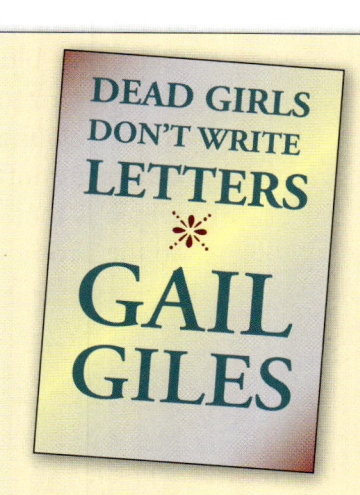

- What do I think of it?

Wow! This is really a good read. Really exciting and full of twists. I liked the idea that the sisters are so different (aren't they often in real life?) and that suddenly the bad one is good too. What do you do if you've always been the good one? I won't tell you the ending, but I can tell you that there are a couple of surprises. And have a look at Giles' next book 'Playing in Traffic', it's a thriller, too.
(Review by Anahita)

---

10 **Expand your notes from Exercise 7 and write a book report. Use the model above to help you.**

Sounds right Stress in compound nouns

11 (31) **In compound words the stress is normally on the first syllable in the word. Underline the syllable which is stressed. Then listen and check.**

| graphic novel | horror story | poetry book | comedy film |

UNIT 5   51

Migration

Key words

migrate	breeding grounds	current	Arctic tern
migratory animals/birds	predators	salmon	ruby-throated
breed	supply	blue whale	hummingbird

1 Read the article and match the headings to the paragraphs.

1 24-hour sunlight   3 The final journey   5 Flying through water
2 North and south   4 Size isn't important

A ☐

Each year blue whales travel thousands of kilometres in search of food. They spend the winter months in the warm waters of the Tropics where many of them give birth to their young. When summer arrives, some of them migrate south to Antarctica, and others go north to the Arctic. All of them are looking for the rich supply of plankton which is found in polar waters. After three or four months of feeding, they swim back to the Tropics.

B ☐

The Pacific salmon are famous for their difficult journeys of hundreds of miles from the ocean to their breeding grounds up American rivers. When they start the journey, their bodies are very strong, but as soon as the salmon leave the sea they stop eating. They swim up-river, fighting against strong currents and jumping up waterfalls. Many are eaten by predators or caught by fishermen. Months later the lucky ones arrive, but they are exhausted. They have just enough energy to lay their eggs and die.

UNIT 5

C ☐
Arctic terns fly an incredible 40,000 km every year as they travel between the North and South poles. They also probably see more daylight than any other animal on earth. In their northern home during the summer, the sun doesn't set, and they experience the same long days in their winter home in Antarctica.

D ☐
They may only weigh a couple of grams but when it comes to long-distance flying, ruby-throated hummingbirds are big birds. Twice a year these amazing creatures take off from the USA on a 2,400 km journey before they finally land in Costa Rica. This journey includes a 960 km, 20-hour non-stop flight across the Gulf of Mexico.

E ☐
They can't fly but that doesn't stop penguins from getting about. They are the only birds that migrate by swimming. Using currents they may migrate from Antarctica as far up the east coast of South America as Rio de Janeiro in Brazil.

Mini-project Research on migratory birds

2 **Choose one of these birds.**

| stork | wild goose | starling | crane | puffin |

Search the internet or a library for information about their migration. Think about the questions below. Write a short paragraph to answer each question.

Where do they live?
Where do they migrate to?
Why do they migrate?
How far do they travel?
What dangers are there on their journey?

UNIT 5

UNIT 6 The main event

1 Listen and read.

In this unit

You learn
- the passive
- make / let / be allowed to
- words for special events

and then you can
- talk about ambition
- say where things are done
- say what people let you do

Wimbledon for free

We asked you to tell us how you enjoy yourself in the school holidays. Nadia Mortimer tells us how she had a good time – working hard!

Are you a tennis fan? Would you like to watch the best players in the world – free? Well, that's what I did last year. How? I became a ball girl! Each year a school is chosen to provide the ball boys and girls (they're called BBGs) for Wimbledon. Last year it was my school, and because I was in Year 10 (and 15 years old) I got the chance to go.

We started training in early February and it went on until the tournament started at the end of June. 'What?' I can hear you thinking, 'Five months training? What's difficult about picking up tennis balls?' Sorry, but you have no idea! When we applied, they made us run for twelve minutes, and then stand completely still for four minutes! Does that sound easy? Try it! (Being a BBG can be dangerous, too. One year, a BBG broke his leg during a match. He finished the match, and then he was taken to hospital! And a few years ago, a BBG was hit by a 200 kph serve from Pete Sampras, the champion at the time – but he smiled and kept going!)

Anyway – I was selected, so I went to Wimbledon and did my stuff. It was brilliant! It was so exciting, being so close to some of my favourite players. I couldn't talk to them really – BBGs aren't allowed to talk to players during the matches – but a couple of players let us come to the changing rooms afterwards. I've got some great autographs, and a few brilliant photographs too.

I wasn't paid and I had to work hard, but I had a fantastic two weeks. Unfortunately, it was my one and only time: this year there are school exams during the tournament (they won't let you be a BBG if you've got exams) and next year I'll be too old. But I'll always have great memories of my BBG days!

2 Circle T (True) or F (False) for the sentences below.

1 Nadia was 10 last year. — T / F
2 She trained for five months to be a BBG. — T / F
3 Being a BBG isn't easy. — T / F
4 A BBG had to go to hospital when a ball hit him. — T / F
5 Nadia talked to some players during the matches. — T / F
6 She's going to be a BBG again this year. — T / F

Get talking   Talking about permission

3 Match the questions and answers. Then listen and check.

1 Why don't you wear jeans to school?
2 Why weren't you at the party?
3 Why don't you take your mobile phone to school?
4 Why isn't there a TV in your bedroom?

a) I wasn't allowed to go.
b) We're not allowed to use them there.
c) I'm not allowed to have one.
d) We're not allowed to wear them.

4 Work with a partner. Use the prompts to make short conversations.

A Are you allowed to .... ?

B Yes, but I'm not allowed to ....

✓ go to parties
✗ come home very late

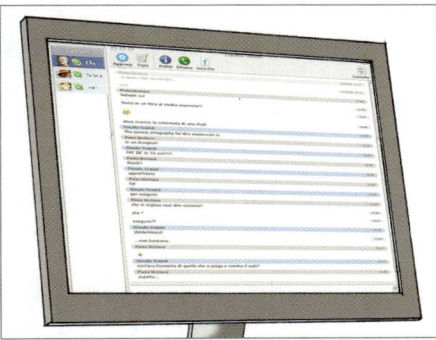

✓ surf the internet
✗ go into chat rooms

✓ buy your own clothes
✗ dye my hair

✓ invite friends over
✗ make a lot of noise

✓ go to fast-food places
✗ eat fast-food every day

UNIT 6   55

Language Focus

Vocabulary Special events

1 Match the words and pictures.

- [ ] book fair
- [ ] rock festival
- [ ] fashion show
- [ ] car show
- [ ] tennis tournament
- [ ] opening night
- [ ] cycling race
- [ ] school fete

2 Where would you expect to find these people?

| actors and actresses | fans | teachers | models |
| sportsmen and women | authors | pop stars | journalists |

Get talking Talking about events

3 Complete the dialogues with the replies. Listen and check.

1 I loved it. I saw Nadal play.
2 Yes, I went to Glastonbury last year.
3 Yes, I went on a school trip to Wimbledon two years ago.
4 It was fantastic. All my favourite bands were there.

A Have you ever been to a rock festival?
B ¹_Yes, I went to Glastonbury last year._
A What was it like?
B ² ....

A Have you ever been to a tennis tournament?
B ³ ....
A What was it like?
B ⁴ ....

4 Work with a partner. Ask each other questions about the events in Exercise 1. Use the dialogues from Exercise 3 to help you.

56 UNIT 6

Grammar

The passive

1 Complete the sentences from the texts on page 54 with the words on the right.

1 Each year a school ....
2 A BBG .... by a 200 kph serve.
3 He .... to hospital.
4 BBGs .... to talk to the players.
5 I .... any money.

was hit
is chosen
aren't allowed
wasn't paid
was taken

The Present simple passive has the following structure:
Subject + Present simple of **be (not) + Past participle**.

2 Read the sentences. Which events are they talking about?

1 The film is shown to a specially invited audience.
2 The cars are washed every morning.
3 The parents of the children are all invited.
4 The race leader wears a yellow shirt.
5 The champion wins over £500,000
6 Bands from all over the UK come to play.

3 Complete the sentences with the Present simple passive form of the verb.

How it Works – A Rock Festival
1 First a big field .... (find) for the event.
2 Then the bands .... (choose) and .... (invite) to play.
3 The festival .... (advertise) on the radio and in the newspapers.
4 Tickets .... (sold) on the internet.
5 A big stage .... (build) in the field.
6 Security .... (organise).
7 The gates .... (open)
8 Finally the fans .... (search) when they arrive.

The Past simple passive has the following structure:
Subject + Past simple of **be (not) + Past participle**.

4 Rewrite the underlined sentences. Use the Past passive.

1 The school fashion show was a great success. [1] They invited 100 people and most of them came. [2] They raised more than £1,000 for charity. It really was a big event and there were even a few famous people there. [3] The photographers took loads of pictures and [4] the newspaper put the show on its front page. The clothes were fantastic. [5] School children designed them all. It was amazing. In fact [6] the teenagers organised the whole evening. [7] A 16 year-old boy wrote the music and [8] a 14 year-old girl did the lights. It was wonderful to see what young people can do.

1 100 people *were invited.*
2 More than £1,000 ....
3 Loads of pictures ....
4 The show ....
5 All the clothes ....
6 ....
7 ....
8 ....

UNIT 6 57

Make / let / be allowed to

5 Complete the sentences from the text on page 54. Use *made / let / allowed*.

1 They .... us run for twelve minutes.
2 BBGs aren't .... to talk to players during the matches.
3 A couple of players .... us come to the changing rooms afterwards.

> **Note**
> The past tense of **let** is **let**

6 Nick is on a camping weekend with the scouts. Write sentences starting with *They make him / don't make him / let him / don't let him…*

1 make / get up / 6 o'clock every morning
   They make him get up at 6 o'clock every morning.
2 not let / stay up later than 10 p.m.
3 make / help to prepare the food.
4 not make / help with the cleaning
5 let / watch the football on TV
6 make / put up his own tent
7 not let / stay in the tent during the day
8 let / use the internet in the camp office

7 Match the signs and the sentences.

A Keep off the grass
B Lights out 11pm
C (no dogs)
D (no mobile phones)
E (do not feed animals)
F (no running)

1 You aren't allowed to keep the lights on after 11 pm.
2 You aren't allowed to take dogs here.
3 You aren't allowed to walk on the grass.
4 You aren't allowed to feed the animals here.
5 You aren't allowed to run here.
6 You aren't allowed to take use mobile phones here.

8 Write sentences using the correct form of *be allowed to*.

1 James ✓ watch TV / ✗ not watch TV after 10 o'clock.
   James is allowed to watch TV but he isn't allowed to watch TV after 10 o'clock.
2 Sarah ✓ go to bed late / ✗ not get up late

3 We ✓ wear jeans to school / ✗ not wear shorts

4 They ✓ listen to music / ✗ not listen without headphones

5 I ✓ go to my friend's house / ✗ not stay overnight

6 She ✓ have parties at home / ✗ not play loud music

58 UNIT 6

Skills

Reading

1 Read the magazine article. Find out what these numbers refer to.

a) over 3 million   b) 200, 000   c) between 1 and 2 million   d) 5,000

Really big events? Rio's the place!

Football crowds

The largest number of people ever at a football match was in 1950 – the final of the World Cup, at the Maracanã Stadium in Rio. The stadium was built especially for the World Cup, and everyone in Brazil was sure that Brazil would win. They got to the final, against Uruguay, and only needed a draw to be the champions. 173,850 people paid to go in and watch, but journalists and officials made the probable number 200,000 or so. But, to the disappointment of the Brazilians, Uruguay won 2-1 to take the World Cup for the second time.

Rock concerts

There have been some enormous rock concerts in Rio. In 1994, Rod Stewart played on the beach in Copacabana on December 31st, and it is estimated that over 3 million people were there – a world record. The Rolling Stones played on the beach just before Carnival in 2006, but they only(!) got about 1.2 million to come out and watch. And there have been 3 'Rock in Rio' festivals, with hundreds of thousand of fans going over 3 or 4 days to watch huge bands like R.E.M., Oasis and Red Hot Chili Peppers.

Carnival

Numbers of people at Carnival are difficult to measure, at least if you're thinking about the number of people in the streets of Rio. But one thing is for sure: the parade of samba schools in the Sambódromo is huge. Each year, over two consecutive nights, the fourteen top samba 'schools' in Rio parade in the stadium. Each school has between 4,000 and 5,000 people, and each school takes 80 minutes to parade. The special stadium, which was built in 1984, holds 65,000 people, but millions of people watch on TV too.

New Year's Eve

New Year's Eve is a big event almost everywhere in the world, but there are very few places where it's bigger than Copacabana. Usually there are between 1 and 2 million people on the beach to watch the fireworks display that begins at midnight. These days, after the fireworks there are usually 2 or 3 simultaneous concerts on the beach with famous musicians. The party goes on, of course, into the daylight hours!

2 Read the text again. Answer the questions.

1. Why was the Maracanã stadium built?
2. Why were the Brazilians disappointed in 1950?
3. Who takes part in the parades in the sambódromo each year?
4. How many people can watch the samba school parade in the sambódromo?
5. How long do 'Rock in Rio' festivals last?
6. What time does the New Year's Eve party finish?

UNIT 6   59

Listening

3 Say the numbers in the table.

20	312,000	687	42,000
140,000	500,000	27,000	2 billion

35 Where do you think the numbers go in the text below? Fill in the gaps, then listen and check.

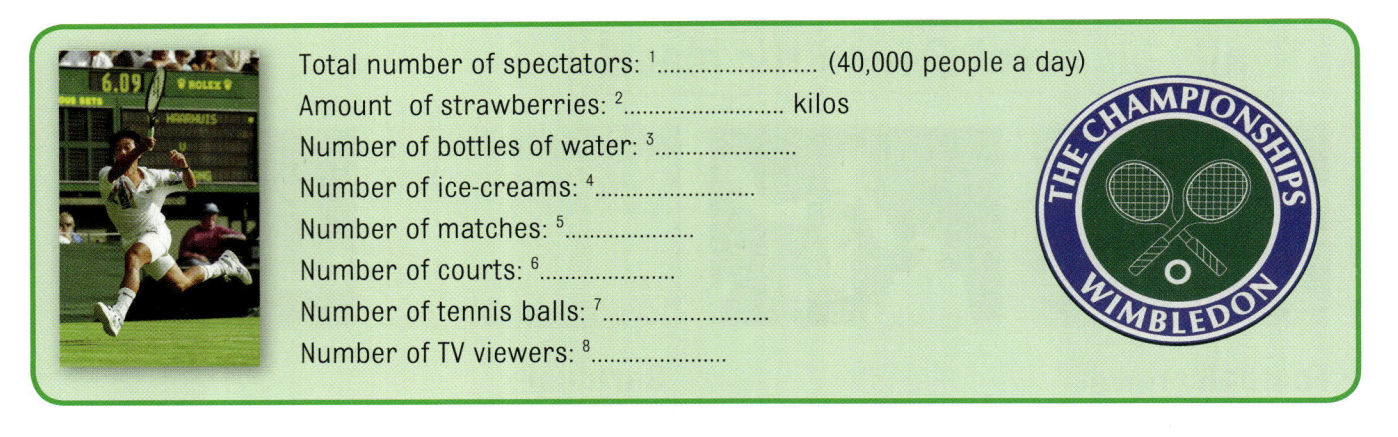

Total number of spectators: ¹......................... (40,000 people a day)
Amount of strawberries: ²......................... kilos
Number of bottles of water: ³.....................
Number of ice-creams: ⁴.........................
Number of matches: ⁵....................
Number of courts: ⁶....................
Number of tennis balls: ⁷.........................
Number of TV viewers: ⁸....................

THE CHAMPIONSHIPS WIMBLEDON

Speaking and listening

4 Listen to a group of students discussing a task and make a note of their answers to the questions.

5 Work in small groups and do the task in Exercise 4. Present your ideas to the class.

You are going to organise an event to raise money for charity.
1 What kind of event are you going to choose?
2 What things do you need to organise?
3 Who is going to do what?
4 How much money do you want to make?
5 What kind of charity are you going to give it to?

Writing

6 Look at Sally's poster for the rock festival. Write a similar poster for your own event.

11A productions proudly present
The St David's Experience
Rock Festival
Featuring:
The Flying Pigs, Overdrive, Skool Rulez and The Henriettas.

When: Saturday July 1st.
Where: School football pitch
Tickets only £5 for the whole day –
See **Leroy Sparks** (11A)

Let us entertain you!

60   UNIT 6

Check your progress Units 5 and 6

1 Complete the words.

1 c _ _ _ _ _ _ _ _ _ of short stories
2 rock f _ _ _ _ _ _ _
3 detective n _ _ _ _
4 fashion s _ _ _
5 school f _ _ _
6 tennis t _ _ _ _ _ _ _ _ _
7 non-f _ _ _ _ _ _ book
8 opening n _ _ _ _

☐ 8

2 Complete the sentences.

1 It's a comedy, it's _ _ _ _ _ _ .
2 It's a sci-fi, it's _ _ _ _ _ _ _ _ _ .
3 It's a _ _ _ _ _ _ _ _ _ _ , it's interesting.
4 It's a horror story, it's _ _ _ _ _ _ .
5 It's a _ _ _ _ _ _ _ _ , it's thrilling.

☐ 5

3 Complete the dialogues. Use the passive (present or past) and *so/such*.

1 **A** This is ¹............... a good book.
    B Who ²............... it .... (write) by?
    A Philip Pullman. It's great. I'm ³............... excited about what happens next.
    B I think that book ⁴............... (chose) for a prize.
    A Yes, it was. He's ⁵............... a good writer!

2 **A** There's a music festival at the weekend. It ⁶............... (advertise) in the local newspaper. There are ⁷............... a lot of famous groups coming!
    B It's ⁸............... wet though. It might not happen.
    A Don't say that! I've already got a ticket! The tickets ⁹............... (sell) online.
    B Were they? I'm ¹⁰............... terrible with computers! I never buy anything online.
    A It's not ¹¹............... a difficult thing to do! Come on! I'll help you!

☐ 11

4 Complete using *so* or *such*.

1 That was .... silly of you.
2 Gemma was .... tired that she went straight to bed.
3 This is .... an interesting book!
4 I have never seen .... a bad film!
5 He's going to buy me a book. That's .... a great idea!

☐ 5

5 Complete the phrasal verbs.

1 I .... into your sister in the street.
2 Oh wow! I love this song! .... it up!
3 Jim's .... up horse riding. He'd never tried it before!
4 Who do you .... after most – your mum or your dad?
5 Billy .... over a glass of water and it went on my palmtop!
6 Sometimes I need to read half of a book before I .... into it.

☐ 6

6 Rewrite the sentences using the Passive.

1 They chose our school to enter the contest.
   ....
2 They always invite parents to the school fete.
   ....
3 A falling light hit a fan at the concert.
   ....
4 They searched the girl.
   ....
5 We organise a party at the end of every year.
   ....

☐ 10

7 Complete using *make, let* or *be allowed*.

1 My teachers .... me do too much work.
2 I .... to go out tonight – Mum said 'No'.
3 They won't .... me watch that film.
4 She .... me try her new shoes.
5 He .... me to drive his car.

☐ 5

TOTAL ☐ 50

My progress so far is …

☺ brilliant! ☐   😐 quite good. ☐   ☹ not great. ☐

UNIT 6   61

Learn MORE about Culture

Marathons!

1 Read the text and decide if the sentences below are T (True) or F (False).

1. You can see the sea when you run the South Devon Coastal Marathon. T / F
2. The Wendover Woods Marathon is easier than most. T / F
3. People run the Baxters Loch Ness Marathon dressed as monsters. T / F
4. There is a marathon where you run on ice. T / F
5. In the marathon in the Himalayas, you have to run up Everest. T / F

> Marathons are run everywhere. There are lots to choose from if you want to see different places. The South Devon Coastal Marathon is run close to the sea. The Wendover Woods Marathon is run up and down steep hills and is challenging. The Salisbury 5-4-3-2-1 Trail Marathon takes you past castles. The Moray Marathon in Scotland is the place for nature lovers as you might see whales and dolphins on the way. Even more exciting than that is the Baxters Loch Ness Marathon, as this takes you past the home of the legendary Loch Ness Monster!
> For people who want to travel further, marathons are also held in the North Pole where you run on ice! In Kenya, you run through a game park with wild animals. There's even a marathon in the Himalayas, however, you don't have to run up Everest.

2 (37) Listen and try to match the people in the London Marathon to the charities they supported. Then listen again and check.

Competitor	Charity
Dressed as a superhero	Maasai Warriors
Wearing a bucket on the head	The Anthony Nolan Trust
Dressed in a heart costume	WaterAid
As themselves	CRY (Cardiac Risk in the Young)

Do YOU know?

Originally, there was no fixed distance for the marathon race. 40 kilometres became the standard until the 1908 Olympic Games in London, where the race was made longer so that members of the royal family could see the start and finish. We use that distance today – 42.195 kilometres.

3 (38) Look at the table below and try and complete the missing words and times. Then listen and check your answers.

Competitor	Time
Fastest ever	[3]..... hours 4 minutes 26 seconds
Fastest woman	[4]..... hours [5]..... minutes 25 seconds
Fastest dressed as [1].......................	3 hours 12 minutes 27 seconds
Fastest dressed as a clown	3 hours [6]..... minutes 4 seconds
Fastest dribbling a basketball	4 hours 30 minutes [7]..... seconds
Fastest in a [2]..................... uniform	5 hours 36 minutes 12 seconds
Slowest ever	[8]..... days 8 hours 29 minutes

4 **Over 2 U!** Imagine you are going to take part in the London Marathon. In groups decide on a charity to raise money for and a costume to wear. Find out about that charity. Write a paragraph about it and present it to the class.

MORE! And now you can watch *School Reporters*!

UNIT 6

Chill out at the Guilfest

Want some ideas for things to do in the summer? Here's my highlight from last July. I went to the Guilfest in Guildford for three days, with my older brother Daniel. What's the Guilfest? A three-day music festival with six separate stages and loads of bands. It started on the Friday and went on for three days. Great bands! I liked Morning Runner, Nizlopi, Gary Numan, Big Wednesday and Billy Idol best. As far as autographs go, I was really successful. I got John and Luke from Nizlopi, and Gary Numan, too.

Daniel's been going to the Guilfest for a couple of years now. He says he's had some great experiences there. Here's an example. The first time Nizlopi came to Guilfest, they played in a tent with about a thousand people in it, all standing up. When they'd been playing for some time, they got off the stage and went down in the middle of the crowd. Suddenly two or three people sat down and then everyone else did the same. Daniel says that it was a really special moment. Everyone kept really quiet, and Daniel says he had the feeling that the band were playing just for him.

We camped at the Guilfest this year and if you have the money, you can rent a camper. If you get tired of listening to the bands, you can walk over to the Guildford outdoor swimming pool and spend some time there.

Four more things I liked about the weekend:

Number 1. There's a big leisure centre nearby. So having a shower's not a problem.

Number 2. Stoke Park, where the festival's held, is a really beautiful place, lots of green.

Number 3. There was a theatre tent, too. We went to Guilfest for the music, of course, but it's nice to do something else occasionally.

Number 4. Last but not least, the toilets were clean (and believe me, at a music festival, that's important!)

So if you want something a bit different to do this year, you could try the Guilfest. Just check out their site on www.guilfest.co.uk, OK?

Read MORE for pleasure

For **MORE!** Go to **www.cambridge.org/elt/more** and do a quiz on this text.

UNIT 6

UNIT 7 Food, glorious food

In this unit

You learn
- will/won't predictions
- question tags (Revision)
- words for food

and then you can
- make offers
- talk about food

1 Listen and read.

Greg Wow – I'm pretty tired. And hungry!

Emily Me too. Let's get some lunch.

Asher Good idea. I'm starving. How about going to Leo's?

Emily Oh, Ash. We always go there. And you always order the baked potato with sour cream filling. Can't we try somewhere else? Please? Just for a change?

Asher That's OK with me, Em. I don't mind where we go. If I'm with you, it'll be great!

Emily Creep!

Greg How about a curry? Look, there's an Indian place right here. I've never eaten curry but I'd sure like to try it.

Emily I'm not sure that's such a good idea, Greg. Indian food's pretty spicy, you know.

Asher It's OK, Em. He doesn't have to order a vindaloo, does he? There'll be lots of things on the menu that aren't too hot.

Emily Maybe – but he said he wants to try curry, didn't he?

Greg Hey – hold on. I'm still here, you know! Look, you two both like Indian food, and I want to try it. So what's the problem?

Emily Sorry Greg – it's just that I'm sure you won't like it. And if you don't enjoy the food, there's no point in going, is there?

Greg I guess not.

Asher Well, let's not stand around here arguing about it. Forget the curry – let's go to Leo's, same as always.

Emily OK. And I'll pay for the meal, OK?

Asher Yes! You won't regret it, Em.

Greg And I'll try curry some other time – when I'm on my own!

2 Write E (Emily), A (Asher) or G (Greg).

1 .... suggests going to Leo's.
2 .... likes baked potatoes with sour cream.
3 .... doesn't want to go the same place again.
4 .... wants to try curry for the first time.
5 .... is sure Greg won't like Indian food.
6 .... says she will pay for lunch.

Get talking Making offers

3 Complete the dialogues with the words from the box. There are two you won't use. Then listen and check.

> make a picnic   do your homework   pay   get the phone   buy a new coat

A Let's go to Leo's Burger Bar.
B Great. I'll ¹.........................

A Let's go to the beach.
B That's a good idea. I'll ².........................

A Let's phone for a pizza.
B OK. I'll ³.........................

4 Match the actions and the pictures.

1 buy flowers
2 eat a sandwich
3 wash the car
4 turn the TV on
5 close the curtains
6 open the window

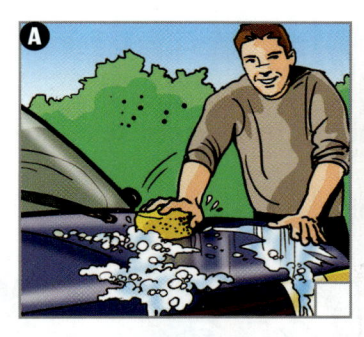

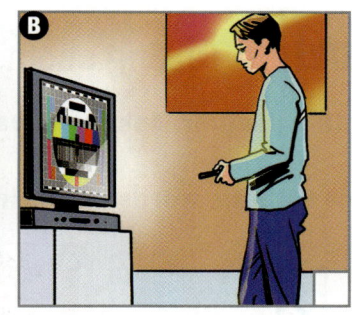

5 Work with a partner. Use the dialogues from Exercise 3 and the prompts below to make mini dialogues.

1 go for a drive tomorrow
2 get some air in this room
3 watch the game
4 get something to eat
5 get Julia a 'thank you' present
6 watch the film in the dark

UNIT 7   65

Language Focus

Vocabulary Food

41 **1** Write the correct number on the left. Then listen and check.

- [ ] grilled fish
- [ ] a raw carrot
- [ ] a baked potato
- [ ] a roast chicken
- [ ] a boiled egg
- [ ] a fried egg

42 **2** Match the questions and answers. Listen and check.

1 How do you like eggs?
2 How do you like potatoes?
3 How do you like carrots?
4 How do you like chicken?

a) I like them raw.
b) I don't. I'm a vegetarian.
c) I like them fried with ketchup.
d) I like them boiled with toast.

Get talking Talking about food

3 Work with a partner. Ask the questions from Exercise 2. Talk about other foods.

4 Complete with the words on the left.

hot
sickly
sweet
sour
~~mild~~
light

1 Curries can be _mild_ or .... !

2 Apples can be .... or .... !

3 Chocolate cake can be .... or .... !

66 UNIT 7

Grammar

Will / won't Predictions

1 **Complete the sentences from page 64 with 'll or won't.**

1 There .... be lots of things on the menu that aren't too hot.
2 If I'm with you, it .... be great!
3 I'm sure you .... like it.
4 You .... regret it, Em.
5 I .... pay for the meal.

2 **Complete the rule with will and won't.**

When we are sure about something in the future, we can use will ('ll) or [1]................ (= will not) plus the infinitive of the verb. In speaking, [2]................ is often shortened to 'll

3 **Complete the sentences with the correct verb from the box.**

| will be | won't be | will have | won't have |

1 Fifty people are coming to the party? That's too many. There .... enough food.
2 Next Monday is a holiday, so we .... any lessons.
3 Hurry up, or we .... late!
4 Let's walk into town. The bus .... a long time.
5 I'm not feeling very well. I think I .... some medicine.
6 We can't visit James tomorrow. We .... enough time.

4 **Complete B's replies with 'll or won't.**

1 **A** I'm going to try eating raw steak.
  B Really? I don't think you .... like it.
2 **A** I don't know how to make curry.
  B Ask Gerry to come round – he .... show you.
3 **A** I feel like a pizza.
  B OK, let's go to La Fornia, I'm sure you .... love their pizzas!
4 **A** I invited Julie to the barbecue tomorrow.
  B Well, she hates meat, so I'm sure she .... come.
5 **A** Don't put salt in the soup.
  B But if I don't, it .... taste horrible.
6 **A** I eat loads of fast food – I love it.
  B Well, you .... be sorry when you're older!

UNIT 7

Question tags (Revision)

5 Complete the question tags. Look at the dialogue on page 64 to check your answers.

1 He doesn't have to order a vindaloo, ………………… he?
2 There's no point in going, ………………… there?
3 He said he wants to try curry, ………………… he?

6 Circle the correct question tag.

1 It's easy, *isn't it* / *doesn't it*?
2 The film was really bad, *wasn't it* / *didn't it*?
3 We aren't late, *aren't we* / *are we*?
4 She lives in that house, *isn't it* / *doesn't she*?
5 You don't like curry, *don't you* / *do you*?
6 You're going to be there, *don't you* / *aren't you*?
7 It won't rain tomorrow, *is it* / *will it*?
8 You know where he lives, *don't you* / *doesn't he*?

7 Complete the question tags.

1 She's French, ………………… she?
2 These apples are delicious, ………………… they?
3 You don't know the answer, ………………… you?
4 Japanese people love good food, ………………… they?
5 The meal wasn't very expensive, ………………… it?
6 You've never eaten Italian food, ………………… you?
7 They didn't like it, ………………… they?
8 You went to Paris last year, ………………… you?

8 Complete the sentences with a question tag.

1 You're Australian, …………………?
2 You don't speak English, …………………? 
3 We're in the wrong place, …………………? 
4 The curry's quite hot, …………………? 
5 You know a lot about animals, …………………? 
6 You aren't a very good dancer, …………………? 

UNIT 7

Skills

Reading

1 Read the text and answer the questions

1. What does Jamie Oliver do?
2. What is strange about the name 'school dinners'?
3. What does 'Feed Me Better' want to do?

Feed me better

Jamie Oliver is a world-famous English chef who owns and runs his own restaurants, and trains new chefs. He also does cookery programmes on television. A few years ago, he did a TV programme called 'Jamie's School Dinners'.

Many schools in Britain give the kids a meal at lunch time – the meals are called 'school dinners' (even though they're lunches, not dinners!). There are people called 'dinner ladies' who make the meals for the kids.

In the programme, Jamie Oliver found that a lot of school dinners are just 'junk food': food which is filling but not very healthy because it has artificial things in it. Since the programme, Jamie has started a movement called 'Feed Me Better', which is trying to improve school dinners.

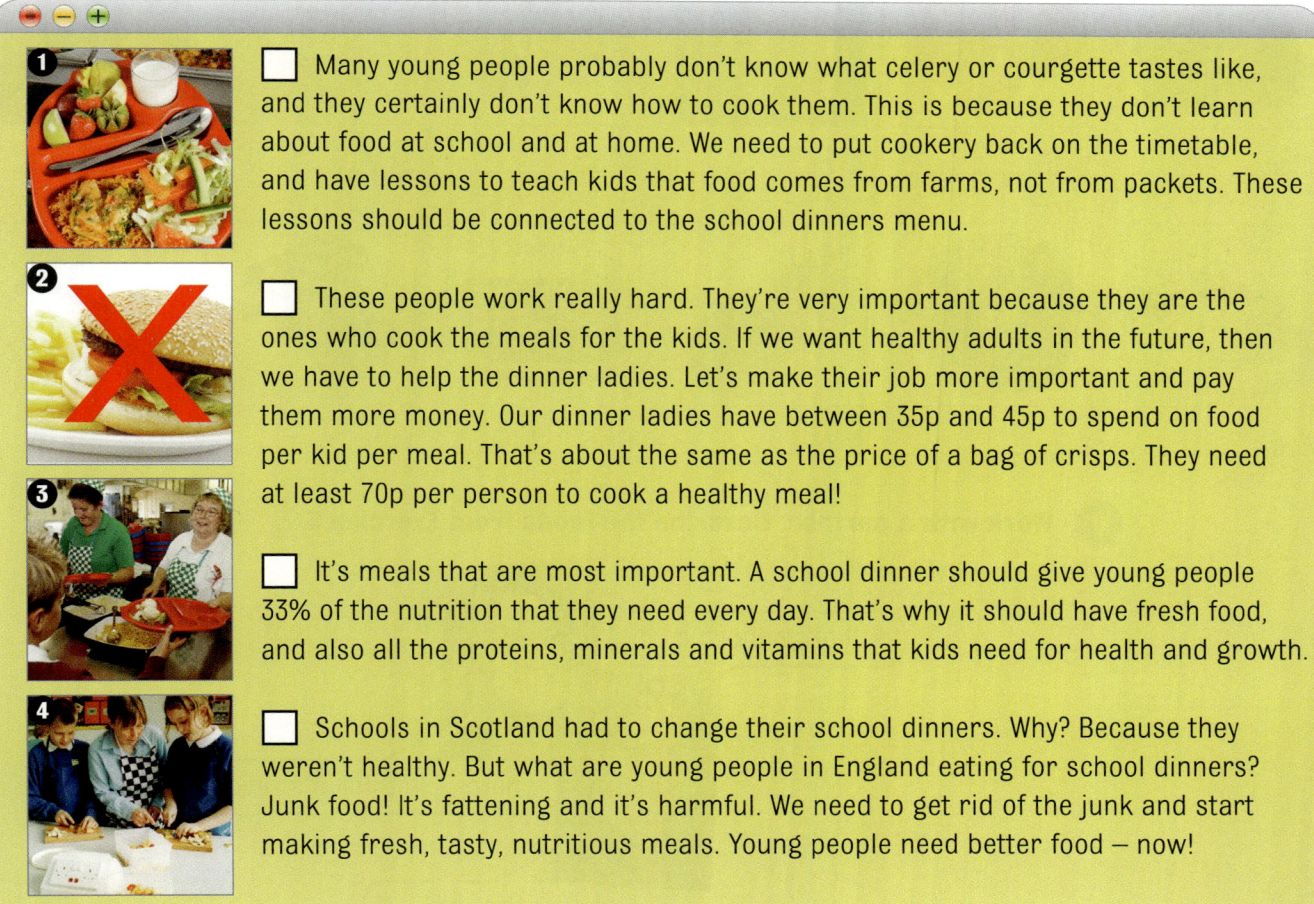

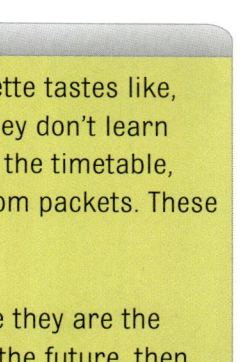

2 Here is a page from the *Feed Me Better* website. Match the texts and pictures.

☐ Many young people probably don't know what celery or courgette tastes like, and they certainly don't know how to cook them. This is because they don't learn about food at school and at home. We need to put cookery back on the timetable, and have lessons to teach kids that food comes from farms, not from packets. These lessons should be connected to the school dinners menu.

☐ These people work really hard. They're very important because they are the ones who cook the meals for the kids. If we want healthy adults in the future, then we have to help the dinner ladies. Let's make their job more important and pay them more money. Our dinner ladies have between 35p and 45p to spend on food per kid per meal. That's about the same as the price of a bag of crisps. They need at least 70p per person to cook a healthy meal!

☐ It's meals that are most important. A school dinner should give young people 33% of the nutrition that they need every day. That's why it should have fresh food, and also all the proteins, minerals and vitamins that kids need for health and growth.

☐ Schools in Scotland had to change their school dinners. Why? Because they weren't healthy. But what are young people in England eating for school dinners? Junk food! It's fattening and it's harmful. We need to get rid of the junk and start making fresh, tasty, nutritious meals. Young people need better food – now!

3 Read the texts again. Answer the questions.

1 Why don't most young people know how to cook things?
2 Why are dinner ladies important?
3 What should school dinners provide?
4 What is more money needed for?

Speaking

4 Match each word with its definition.

1 artificial   a) has good effects on your body
2 harmful   b) makes you become heavier
3 healthy   c) full of the natural things your body needs
4 nutritious   d) not natural; man-made
5 fresh   e) tastes very, very good
6 tasty   f) makes you feel full, feel that you have eaten a lot of food
7 revolting   g) new; not frozen or in a tin
8 filling   h) has bad effects; doesn't do you good
9 fattening   i) tastes very, very bad

5 Look at the food below. Write the names.

1 s......  2 o......  3 m......  4 b......  5 y......  6 s......

7 c......  8 c......  9 p......  10 h......  11 c......  12 c......

6 Work with a partner. Describe the foods from Exercise 5.

I think yoghurt is …

I hate …! I think it's revolting.

Yes, but it's ….

Listening

7 Listen to the radio programme. Number the cities in order of how healthy they are (1 = most healthy → 5 = least healthy).

A Liverpool
B Manchester 
C Bradford 
D Southampton 
E London 

8 Listen again. Correct each sentence.

1 The government has done a report on Fat Britain.
2 The report says that people eat too many vegetables.
3 There was one southern city in the top ten unhealthiest cities.
4 Southampton is in the north of England.
5 London was the fittest city in the UK for the last five years.
6 Experts say the government can control what people eat.

Writing for your Portfolio

9 Read the text. Do you think Paul has a healthy diet? Give reasons.

I often miss breakfast. I'm not very hungry in the morning. But I usually take some fresh fruit with me to school, like an apple or banana, that I can eat in the break. I have lunch at school – it's usually something with chips, a hamburger perhaps or some chicken nuggets. Not very nutritious, I know. When I get home in the afternoon my mum makes me something like a cheese sandwich. In the evening we usually all have dinner at different times – I have something like sausages and chips, normally, but sometimes spaghetti with tomato sauce.

10 Write a short text about what you eat.

Sounds right Question intonation

11 Look back at the questions in Exercise 8, page 68. Practise saying the questions as if you already know the answer (giving an opinion with a falling tone at the end) and then as a real check question (with a rising tone at the end). Then test your partner.

UNIT 7   71

Musical styles

Key words

performer emerge movement breakdancing
producer moody graffiti decline

1 Read the texts. Which of these musical styles do you know about/like?

One of the most popular films of the late 1970s was *Saturday Night Fever*. It told the story of a young dancer played by John Travolta and showed that disco music was big business. Disco had first started a few years earlier with performers such as Donna Summer, The Bee Gees, and Sister Sledge. However, the real stars were the producers of the records who often wrote and created the songs. By the end of the decade 'disco' was popular all over the world. It started to decline in popularity in the early 1980s.

Britpop was a musical style that emerged in the UK in the mid 1990s. It was influenced by the British guitar pop music of the 1960s and bands like The Kinks, The Who and the Beatles. Britpop groups wrote songs about a very British way of life. The media were very quick to identify this new sound which was part of a movement called 'Cool Britannia'. This included a new generation of British artists and fashion designers. By the end of the decade the movement was over although many Britpop bands such as Oasis, Blur and Pulp continued to enjoy success into the new millennium.

If one CD defines early 1990s rock music then it must be Nirvana's *Nevermind*. Suddenly music magazines all over the world were writing about a new sound that was coming from the north American city of Seattle: grunge. Grunge is a style of alternative music influenced by punk, heavy metal and indie rock. The music is often dark and moody. It became very popular with many teenagers who felt it illustrated their lives. Now grunge has lost a lot of its popularity, but many of the original bands such as Pearl Jam, Mudhoney and Alice in Chains continue to attract new teenage audiences.

During the mid 1970s a new music started in the black neighbourhoods of American cities: hip hop (or rap). By 1979 it had become very successful and songs like *Rapper's Delight* by *The Sugarhill Gang* were big hits in many countries. The music consists of two parts; DJing (producing and scratching) and rapping (speaking along to the music). However, hip hop is not just about music – breakdancing and graffiti are also important parts of the culture. These days hip hop is still popular with artists like Eminem, Missy Elliott, Kanye West and Timberland enjoying huge success all over the world.

72 UNIT 7

Music

2 Work in groups. What kind of music do you think these musicians play?

| punk | the blues | pop | heavy metal | techno | country |

3 Listen to the extracts of songs. Which style of music are they?

1 ....
2 ....
3 ....
4 ....
5 ....
6 ....

Discuss with your group:

- what the music sounds like
- where it came/comes from
- when it was popular
- some of the performers associated with it

Mini-project Battle of the Bands

4 Research your favourite band and write a report about them.

Include:
- what style of music they play
- a note on similar bands
- a look at some of the bands who influenced them
- some photographs

5 Present your report in class and play an example of some of their music.

UNIT 7   73

UNIT 8 Body talk

1 Read the texts and match with the photos.
(Careful – one text doesn't have a photo!)

In this unit

You learn
- *could, might, may* for speculation
- *-ed* vs *-ing* adjectives
- words for body movement

and then you can
- talk about emotions
- talk about body movements

A If you show the soles of your feet or shoes in Thailand, people could find it insulting. The soles are the lowest part of the body, so people think they are 'dirty'.

B Do you smile when you want to greet someone in a friendly way? In some cultures people don't smile in this situation, and in others people smile for different reasons. The Japanese, for example, may smile when they are confused or angry.

C In the Middle and Far East, it is not polite to point with your index finger. You should only point with an open hand (or your thumb in Indonesia), never with your index finger.

D Every culture has a 'comfort zone' for personal space when people talk to one another. For Western Europeans and Americans, a distance between people of 35 – 50 cm is comfortable. In the UK, people prefer a little more distance (60 cm); in Japan, even more (90 cm). People in the Middle East may feel strange if the person they're talking to keeps so far away: they prefer shorter distances of 20 – 25 cm.

E You might find it interesting to know that in the Middle and Far East, you should never pass something to another person with your left hand. People think the left hand is 'unclean'. In Japan, use both hands.

F Do you think nodding your head up and down means 'yes' all over the world? You might be surprised if you go to Greece or Bulgaria. In those countries, nodding means 'No'!

74 UNIT 8

2 Write the name of the correct country.

In which country (or countries):
1 should you use your thumb to point? ....
2 do people think the bottom of the foot is not clean? ....
3 might people smile if they don't understand something? ....
4 should you always use two hands to give someone something? ....
5 should you not get much closer than 1m to someone? ....
6 could a 'yes' be mistaken for a 'no'? ....

Get talking Talking about emotions

3 Match the emotions to the correct picture.

disappointed   frightened   bored   tired   excited   interested

A   B    C    D    E    F

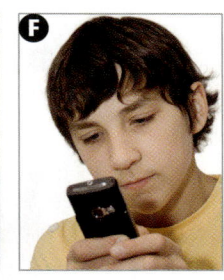

4 Listen and repeat.

A I didn't really like the talk. I thought it was boring.
B Really? I wasn't bored at all.

A I thought the football game was really exciting.
B Really? I didn't find it exciting at all.

5 Work with a partner. Use the prompts to make similar dialogues.

1 horror film / frightening
2 documentary / interesting 
3 book / disappointing 
4 walk / tiring 

UNIT 8   75

Language Focus

Vocabulary Body movements

1 Match the gestures to the pictures.

1 fold your arms   2 cross your legs   3 nod your head   4 scratch your head
5 shake your head   6 wave   7 point a finger   8 shake hands

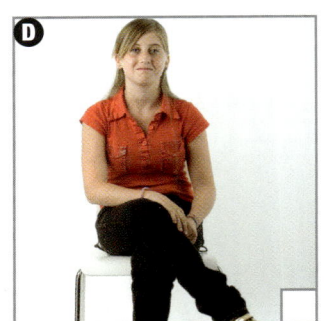

A   B   C   D
E   F   G   H

Get talking Talking about body movements

2 Complete the sentences.

1 I usually f............................ my arms when I'm angry with someone.
2 I always c............................ my legs when I sit.
3 I always w............................ when I say goodbye to my mum in the mornings.
4 I never p............................ I think it's rude.
5 I always s............................ hands when I meet a new person.
6 I s............................ my head when I want to say yes.
7 I sometimes n............................ my head when I agree with someone.
8 I only s............................ my head when I think.

3 Work with a partner. Are these sentences true for you? Say if they are different.

I fold my arms when I'm waiting.

I don't think pointing is rude.

I usually kiss on the cheek when I meet a new person.

76   UNIT 8

Grammar

Could, might, may for speculation

1 Look at the examples from the text on page 74.

1 If you show the soles of your feet or shoes in Thailand, people **could** find it insulting.
2 People in the Middle East **might** feel strange if the person they're talking to keeps far away.
3 The Japanese, for example, **may** smile when they are confused or angry.

Match the meanings of the words *may*, *might* and *could* in the sentences above with a–c.
a) It's possible that   b) It's definite that   c) It's definitely not

Rule
We can use *could*, *might* and *may* to talk about possible situations and hypothesise about a situation. As always, these modal verbs are followed by the infinitive without *to*.

2 Complete the sentences with the words on the right.

1 He's speaking Spanish so he .... from Argentina.
2 Look at the sky. It .... later.
3 They're not playing so well. I think they .... if they're not careful.
4 It's a difficult exam but she .... if she studies really hard.
5 Look in the kitchen. You .... your keys there.
6 I'm so tired I .... asleep in the middle of the film.

could be
could pass
may find
might fall
might rain
may lose

3 Look at the photos. Which parts of the body are they? Choose from the words on the right and write sentences.

1 *It could be hair.*   2 ....   3 ....   4 ....

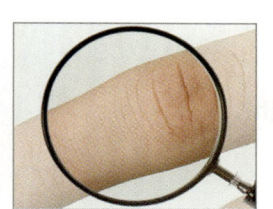

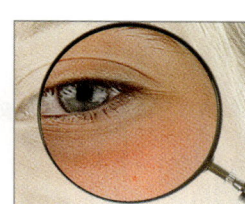

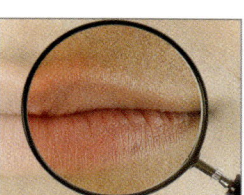

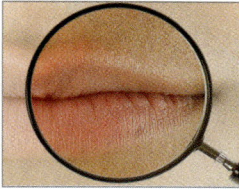

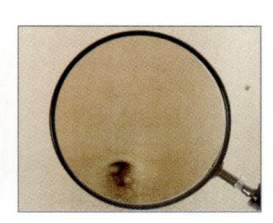

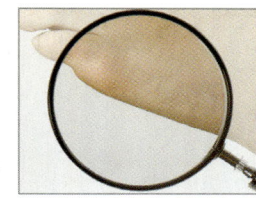

5 ....   6 ....   7 ....   8 ....

mouth
ear
stomach
hair
throat
finger
eye
foot

4 Rewrite the sentences using the words in brackets.

1 Ask Joe. It's possible he knows the answer. (may) ....
2 I'm not sure. It's possibly a problem with your Internet provider. (might) ....
3 She's very upset. It's possible she'll start crying. (may) ....
4 That wall looks very unsafe. It's possible it'll fall down anytime. (could) ....

UNIT 8   77

-ed vs -ing adjectives

5 Look at the examples from the text on page 74 and underline the adjectives.

1 .... people could find it insulting.
2 The Japanese, for example, may smile when they are confused.
3 You might find it interesting to know.
4 It is a rude sign in some cultures and people might be insulted.

Rule
Some adjectives have two forms; *bored/boring, confused/confusing, surprised/surprising* etc.
Generally we use the –ed adjective to describe the feeling we have.
I'm tired (I want to sleep)
We use the –ing adjective to describe the things that produces that feeling.
The walk was tiring (it made me tired)

6 Write the sentences on the right under the correct picture.

1  .... 2  .... 3 ....

4  .... 5  .... 6 ....

He's bored
It's amazing
It's frightening
He's frightened
He's amazed
He's boring

7 Complete the sentences with the words on the right.

1 It's 6pm and Dave's still not home. I'm a bit ....
2 All I got were some socks for my birthday. It was so ....
3 I don't like the way you are talking to me. I find it ....
4 If you're so ...., why don't you go to bed?
5 I met Wayne Rooney! It was the most .... day of life. He's so great.
6 I don't want to go to the museum. I'm not really .... in old cars.

worried
insulting
disappointing
interested
exciting
tired

8 Circle the correct word.

1 I hate football. I find it so *bored/boring*.
2 No-one came to my party. I was so *disappointed/disappointing*.
3 I still get really *excited/exciting* at Christmas.
4 Have you read this article about nano-technology? It's *fascinated/fascinating*.
5 I didn't sleep well at all last night. I'm so *tired/tiring* today.
6 I've got an important exam tomorrow and I'm a little *worried/worrying* about it.
7 I can't find my phone. It's a bit *worried/worrying*.
8 Here's your present. I hope you're not *disappointed/disappointing* by it.

Skills

Reading

1 Read the text. Who lived longer ago, Ötzi or Sir Walter Raleigh?

A short history of piercing

The trendy ice man

What does Ötzi (the mummy found a few years ago near the Austrian-Italian border) have in common with people who want to be trendy? Body piercing! The 'ice man' from about 4,000 years ago had pierced ears!

Piercing in the ancient world

In the ancient world, body piercing was often a symbol of courage and class. That's why it was popular with the Pharaohs in Egypt and with important people in ancient Rome. Tongue piercing was part of a religious ritual of the high priests of the Aztecs. They believed that if their tongues were pierced, they could communicate better with the gods.

Piercing in Africa and Central America

In some areas of these continents, people believed that demons could enter the body through the ears. So they pierced their ears and put ornaments in. They thought that the metal would stop demons from getting into the body.

Piercing in the time of Queen Elizabeth I

In Elizabethan England, a lot of famous men like Shakespeare, Sir Walter Raleigh and Sir Francis Drake wore gold rings in their ears. In those days, sailors also wore earrings, for two reasons: firstly, they thought they could see better if their ears were pierced; and secondly, they thought, 'If our ship sinks and we die, and our bodies are found on the beach, the gold earrings will pay for our funeral.'

Piercing today

In the United States in the 1960s, body piercing became a form of rebellion for young people. Later, it lost its rebellious meaning and just became fashionable: because more and more film stars and sports stars were getting pierced, young people wanted to imitate them.

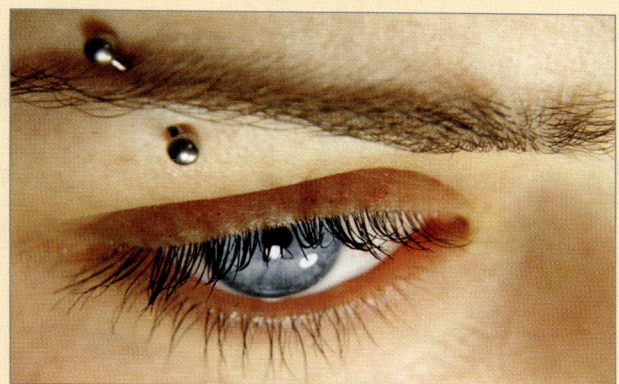

2 Read the text again and complete the table.

Who?	Where?	Why?
Ötzi	ears	Reason not given
Aztec priests		
Africans		
Elizabethan sailors		
Young Americans in the 1960s		

UNIT 8 79

Listening and speaking

3 *Fantastic Voyage* is a cult film from 1966. Listen to the story and find two mistakes in the picture.

4 Listen again. Match the sentence halves to make a summary of the story.

1 Fantastic voyage is set
2 An important scientist is
3 The Fantastic Voyage is
4 A miniature submarine travels
5 The submarine has
6 This crew includes
7 The mission can't
8 One of the crew is

a) dying from a blood clot.
b) in the blood stream to reach his brain.
c) trying to destroy the mission.
d) a journey inside his body.
e) a crew of five people.
f) a pilot, a doctor and his assistant, a bloodstream expert and an agent.
g) in the cold war.
h) take longer than an hour.

5 Work in groups. Discuss the questions and make up your own ending to the story. Then tell your stories to the rest of the group and vote on the best one.

1 How does the submarine get into the body?
2 What obstacles do they meet inside the body?
3 Who is trying to destroy the mission and why?
4 How do they discover who it is?
5 How do they break up the clot?
6 Do they get out in time?
7 Is the mission a success?
8 What happens due to this mission?

6 Read the DVD review of *Fantastic Voyage*. Tick the things that the critic likes.

☐ the story   ☐ the special effects   ☐ the actors
☐ the music   ☐ the dialogue

Classic DVDs

Fantastic Voyage is a great adventure film for all the family that is as entertaining today as it was forty years ago. It's true that the special effects are a bit out-of-date but that helps give the film its appeal. The story is great. It involves a mission inside the human body to save the life of a scientist who can save the world. It's exciting and keeps you watching until the very end of the film. It also stars some of the great screen icons of the 1960's; Raquel Welch, Stephen Boyd and Donald Pleasence. Highly recommended.

Writing for your Portfolio

7 Write a mini review of an old film you have seen.

UNIT 8

Check your progress Units 7 and 8

1 Complete the words.

1 r_ _ eggs/meat/vegetables
2 f_ _ _ _ potatoes/chicken/eggs
3 b_ _ _ _ _ vegetables/eggs
4 g_ _ _ _ _ _ fish/meat
5 r_ _ _ _ meat/chicken/potatoes
6 f_ _ _ your arms
7 c_ _ _ _ your legs
8 n_ _ or s_ _ _ _ _ _ your head
9 s_ _ _ _ hands / your head

☐ 10

2 Write sentences with the correct adjective.

1 She /interest /in film
....
2 He / very insult
....
3 It's a /fright/ DVD
....
4 They /worry/ about their exams
....
5 It's a /disappoint/ result
....
6 The instructions are /confuse
....

☐ 12

3 Complete the dialogue with the correct question tag or adjective.

A I'm really ¹.................. (boring). There's nothing to do!
B It's half past 3, ².................. ? There's a space documentary on Sky.
A Let's watch it! You like space things, ³.................. ?
B Yes, I love them. They're ⁴.................. (fascinate).
A You've got lots of books about space, ⁵.................. ?
B Well, I haven't —my brother has. But, yes, space is ⁶.................. (amaze)!

☐ 6

4 Write the question tags.

1 John isn't coming to your party, ...
2 It was Karen who bought the flowers, ...
3 John and David aren't brothers, ...
4 Jeannette goes to school with you, ...
5 We don't have to tell anyone, ...
6 You won't forget, ...

☐ 6

5 Write sentences using could, may or might. Use the words in brackets.

1 Don't speak like that. You will insult people.
   If you ....
   (be insulted)
2 People in the UK stand further away from each other.
   People in the UK ....
   (uncomfortable / stand too close)
3 He's speaking French. Maybe he's from France.
   He's speaking ....
   (so he)
4 The sky is black. There's a chance that it will rain later.
   The sky .... (so it)
5 You need to do more work or you will fail the exam.
   If you don't ....
   (fail)
6 I think there is more information about this on the Internet.
   You ....
   (find)
7 Perhaps this piece of metal is from a UFO!
   This .... (be from)
8 Take it back to the shop. Maybe they will give you your money back.
   They ....
   (if you ask)

☐ 16

TOTAL ☐ 50

My progress so far is ...

☺ brilliant! ☐   😐 quite good. ☐   ☹ not great. ☐

UNIT 8   81

Learn MORE about Culture

Street performers!

1 Read about a festival in Canada and answer the questions.

Do you know?

The British word for *street performer* or *street musician* is *busker*. The word *busker* was first used in the English language in the 1860s. The word *busk* comes from the Spanish root word *buscar*, which means 'to look for'. And buskers are of course looking for fame and fortune. The actor Robin Williams and the rock star Eric Clapton both started their careers as buskers.

The Edmonton International Street Performers' Festival is Canada's oldest street theatre festival. It has been held since 1983 in the city of Edmonton. Every year, over 50 of the world's best street performers take part in the festival.

During the festival, you can watch comedians, actors, clowns, musicians and masked characters walk around the festival site and entertain their audience. All the entertainment is free.

In the first year of the festival there was a performer called Philippe Petit – a French high-wire artist. This daring man had become famous in 1974 when he illegally put a wire between the World Trade Centre Towers and walked across it – 400 metres above the streets of New York City. In Canada, he walked from the fifth floor of one building to the eleventh floor of another.

Apart from the street entertainment, there is another side to the festival. As part of the Comedy Cares programme, performers use their amazing talents in local hospitals to make patients, family and staff laugh.

1. Where is Edmonton?
2. Who takes part in the Edmonton festival?
3. How much does it cost to see each performance?
4. Where did Philippe Petit perform his most daring high-wire walk?
5. Where is the Comedy Cares programme performed?

2 Listen to the interview with Karen, a human statue. Then circle T (True) or F (False).

1. You must not scare anyone. T / F
2. Design your costume to look like a statue you see in a park or museum. T / F
3. Choose a dark brown or green colour for your make up and costume. T / F
4. Stand on something so that you are taller than the crowd. T / F
5. Learn to move slowly like a robot. T / F

3 **Over 2 U!** In groups, design a human statue for your town. Answer these questions.

Where will the statue stand? What will it look like? What will you use to make the costume? What will the statue do to entertain people?

MORE! And now you can watch *School Reporters!*

UNIT 8

It must be her age

When Mum and I came into the sitting room, Aunt Nancy sighed and Uncle Jack looked at me and shouted, 'Look, it's Dracula's daughter!' And then he laughed like mad. I ignored them and walked across their horrible orange carpet to the sofa. From there I could see myself in the mirror.

I looked cool. I looked Goth. Black clothes, fishnet stockings, heavy boots. White face, black eyeliner, black lipstick. Totally, totally Goth. They all looked at me. Mum said, 'It's her age, you know. It's a phase.' Aunt Nancy smiled sadly and Uncle Jack said, 'Does it speak?' 'Ha-ha!' I said. 'Yes, I can hear and speak.' 'Good,' he said, 'because with all that black stuff round your eyes, you probably can't see.' He looked at Mum and his wife for some applause, and they both giggled.

'I hope she doesn't look like that on the wedding day,' Aunt Nancy said. 'Joy wouldn't want her to look like that.' 'Oh no,' Mum said quickly. 'She'll wear the dress Joy bought for her. Won't you, Felicity?' 'Mum, please!' I said. 'Sorry, Flicka – as she likes to be called now', Mum said to Aunt Nancy. 'And what's that on its neck?' Uncle Jack shouted. 'A tattoo,' I said. 'A tattoo of a spider's web.' 'Not a real one!' Mum said, hastily again. 'It's a wash-off one.' 'Wash-off, eh?' my uncle said.

I ignored him. I was embarrassed. I would have liked a real tattoo and not my wash-off one. I didn't say anything for the rest of the evening.

The dress Joy gave me was terrible. All violet and white and cute. But I've always liked my cousin Joy. 'I know I'm asking a lot, but I really want you to wear it for the wedding,' Joy said. 'You're my bridesmaid and I want everything to be just right.'

On the day of the wedding, I felt terrible. But Joy looked really happy, so I tried to smile too. Everyone was wearing suits and flowery dresses – yuck. And then I saw a decent-looking boy. He had a suit and short hair, but he didn't look bad. Not bad at all.

A few minutes later he walked over to me. 'Cousin of the bride?' he said. 'Yes,' I said. 'And who are you?' 'I'm Lawrence. Cousin of the bridegroom.'

Goth

Read MORE for pleasure

For **MORE!** Go to www.cambridge.org/elt/more and do a quiz on this text.

UNIT 9 Fame

In this unit

You learn
- *used to* (Revision)
- gerunds after prepositions
- words for award shows

and then you can
- talk about past and present favourites
- talk about awards

1 Listen and read.

Greg I'm thinking of staying in tonight. Is there anything worth watching on TV?

Emily Of course! The Brits are on!

Greg The what?

Asher The Brits. It's an awards ceremony. They're awards for British musicians.

Greg You mean like the Grammies? That's our music award show in the States. I used to watch it back in the States.

Asher Oh? So, you're into watching award shows? Well, I'm sure you'll enjoy the Brits, too.

Emily So who do you think's going to win, Ash?

Asher I don't know. I'm not very good at predicting things. But the Scissor Sisters might get best group.

Emily No way. The Kaiser Chiefs will definitely win that.

Greg Who are they?

Emily The Kaiser Chiefs! They're really famous. Don't you know 'Every day I love you less'?

Greg Oh, yeah, I know that song. But I didn't know it was the Kaiser Chiefs.

Emily Unbelievable! Asher, can I borrow your MP3 player, please?

Asher What's wrong with yours?

Emily I left it at home. And I need to give Greg a lesson in British music.

Asher Here you are. But I haven't got any Kaiser Chiefs on it any more. I took it all off.

Emily What?

Asher Yeah, that's right. I mean, I used to like them. The early stuff was good. But I've gone off them now.

Greg So who do you like these days?

Asher Stuff like Kanye West and Beyoncé.

Greg Now *that's* what I call good music!

2 Circle the correct word.

1 The Brit awards are for *pop stars / actors*.
2 The Grammies is *a British / an American* award ceremony.
3 Asher thinks the *Scissor Sisters / Kaiser Chiefs* will win the best group award.
4 'Every day I love you less' is a song by the *Scissor Sisters / Kaiser Chiefs*.
5 *Emily / Asher* left *her / his* MP3 player at home.
6 Emily wants to tell Greg about *an MP3 player / British music*.
7 Asher *has never liked the Kaiser Chiefs / liked the Kaiser Chiefs in the past*.
8 Greg *likes / doesn't like* Kanye West.

Get talking Talking about past and present favourites

3 Put the dialogues in the correct order. Then listen and check.

A ...... Don't you like *Coldplay* any more?
  ..1.. Who's your favourite band?
  ...... I used to like them, but now I prefer the *Scissor Sisters*.
  ...... I think it's the *Scissor Sisters*.

B ...... Don't you like Brad Pitt any more?
  ...... I think it's Vince Vaughan.
  ...... I used to like him, but now I prefer Vince Vaughan.
  ...... Who's your favourite actor?

C ...... I used to like that, but now I prefer watching TV.
  ...... What's your favourite pastime?
  ...... Don't you like playing computer games any more?
  ...... I think it's watching TV.

4 Complete the chart.

	In the past	Now
My favourite actress		
My favourite singer		
My favourite pastime		
My favourite weekend activity		

5 Work with a partner. Use the chart and make similar dialogues to Exercise 3.

Language Focus

Vocabulary Award shows

1 Look at the words below. Say if they describe an award ceremony, films or music.

| solo male artist | picture | actress | solo female artist |
| group | album | animated film | actor | single |

Get talking Talking about awards

2 Which awards in Exercise 1 could these people or films win?

A Robbie Williams

B *Spiderman III*

C Angelina Jolie

D Beyoncé

E The Rolling Stones

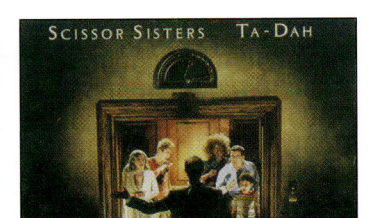

F *Ta-Dah* by the Scissor Sisters

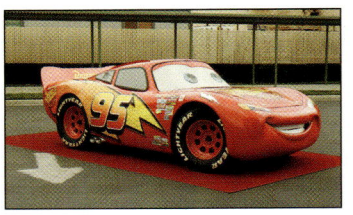

G *Cars*

H Brad Pitt

I *Crazy* by Gnarls Barkley

> **A** Robbie Williams. Is he an actor?

> **B** No, he's a singer. He could win best solo male artist.

3 Listen and check your answers.

4 Work in groups of four. You are going to give the award in each of the categories above.

> **A** And my winner for this category is Jamie Cullum.

> **B** And the winner for the best solo male artist of last year is James Blunt.

Grammar

Used to (Revision)

1 Look at the example sentences from page 84 and answer the questions.

I **used to watch** the Grammies back in the States. (Greg)
I **used to like** the Kaiser Chiefs. (Asher)

1 Does Greg still watch the Grammies?
2 Does Asher still like the Kaiser Chiefs?

To talk about past habits we can use *used to* + the infinitive
I **used to** love the Teletubbies.
I **didn't use to** watch any TV.
Did you **use to** watch a lot of TV?

2 Write sentences about Asher.

1 *He used to play piano but now he plays guitar.*
2 ....
3 ....
4 ....
5 ....
6 ....

3 Put the words in order.

1 York / I / to / live / used / New / in
2 school / I / didn't / to / like / use
3 star / to / used / a / She / film / be
4 me / use / They / to / like / didn't
5 same / she / to / as / go / you / Did / to / the / use / school?

4 Work with a partner. Ask and answer questions.

When you were seven did you use to:
1 watch cartoons?
2 walk to school on your own?
3 like vegetables?
4 spend all your pocket money on sweets?

A Yes, I did and I still do.
B No, I didn't.

UNIT 9

Gerunds after prepositions

5 Match the beginnings and endings.

1 Greg is thinking of …	watching award shows.
2 He's into …	predicting things.
3 Asher's not very good at …	staying in.

6 Circle the correct options to complete the rule.

Many verbs and adjectives are followed by *an adjective / a preposition*. If we want to use a verb after the preposition, the verb is in the *infinitive / -ing* form.

7 Complete the sentences with the phrases from the box.

on doing   of sitting   on playing   in buying   to going   at reading

1 Jane wasn't keen …………………… parachute jumping.
2 They were interested …………………… a bigger car. 
3 Brian was hopeless …………………… maps. 
4 He's too fond …………………… in the sun 
5 She's looking forward …………………… to Spain tomorrow. 
6 She insisted …………………… the violin. 

8 Complete each sentence with the correct preposition and form of the verb in brackets.

1 My brother's really good …………………… models. (make)
2 I'm hopeless …………………… computers. (use)
3 My friends are thinking …………………… a party next weekend. (have)
4 My uncle's coming next week – I'm looking forward …………………… him again. (see)
5 I've never really been interested …………………… to other countries. (travel)
6 It was very boring, but he insisted …………………… me the whole story. (tell)
7 My parents are really keen …………………… to Peru for their next holiday. (go)
8 I don't like playing football very much, but I'm really …………………… it. (watch)

88   UNIT 9

Skills

Reading

1 Read the article. Write the paragraph headings in the correct places.

| The law | Charity work | Money |

Famous... but are they happy?

Wouldn't we all like to be famous? With a lot of money, freedom, power and respect? And fans – people who love you. But many famous people are not very happy. Why is that?

A ....

When you become famous, many things change in your life. Usually, you get rich. And sometimes very rich people do strange things with their money.
In November 2000, Elton John was asked in a British court if it was true that he had spent a lot of money on flowers between January 1996 and September 1997. John replied: 'Yes, I like flowers.' How much did he spend? £263,000.

B ....

Sometimes we think that famous people have more freedom than ordinary people. That's not really true – but there are some famous people who think the law is not for them.
A lot of stars forget that they cannot just do whatever they want. Winona Ryder learned the lesson. She tried to steal expensive designer clothes from a shop in Beverly Hills. She was in all the newspapers and on all the TV news programmes. Now she isn't as successful as she used to be.

C ....

Some stars use their fame in a positive way, because they understand that they can use their power to make the world a better place. Take the example of film star Angelina Jolie. When she was making a film in Cambodia, she met a lot of people who had to leave their homes. Now Angelina does charity work in several countries, meeting and helping as many people as she can.

2 Read the text again and decide if the sentences are T (True) or F (False).

1 Elton John spent £263,000 on flowers in one year. T / F
2 Winona Ryder tried to steal expensive clothes. T / F
3 Angelina Jolie saw a film about poor people in Cambodia. T / F
4 Angelina Jolie does charity work in seven countries. T / F

Listening

3 **Listen to Paul talking about famous people. Circle the correct answers.**

1 **Paul** The person I want to meet most is …

Shakira   Madonna   Jennifer Lopez

because:
- a) I'm a fan of her music.
- b) I think she's a great person.
- c) she has done a lot for other people.
- d) she's beautiful.

2 The two questions I want to ask her are:
- a) Where do you get the ideas for your songs from?
- b) What was life like for you when you were a teenager?
- c) Have you ever been poor?
- d) Do you like being famous?

4 **Now listen to Annie. Complete the notes.**

Prince Harry   Steven Spielberg   Bill Gates

Annie The person I want to meet most is ....
because ....

The two questions I want to ask him are:
1 ....
2 ....

Writing for your Portfolio

5 **Read the profile of Shaun White.**

All about Shaun White
- He is a professional snowboarder and skateboarder.
- He was born on September 3rd 1986 in San Diego, California.
- Shaun started snowboarding when he was six.
- He has won a lot of gold medals in the X-games.
- He won an Olympic gold medal in Turin 2006.
- His fans call him the 'flying tomato' because he's got long red hair.

6 **Think of a famous person you admire. Write a profile like the one above.**

A Song 4 U Fame

7 Listen and sing. Tick the things mentioned in the song.

1 Fame is free. ☐
2 Fame lives forever. ☐
3 Fame is easily forgotten. ☐
4 Fame lights up the sky. ☐
5 Fame makes people love you. ☐
6 Fame can catch the moon. ☐
7 Fame can break your heart. ☐
8 Fame is tough. ☐

Reading and writing

8 Now read the text about Shaun. What information from the profile in Exercise 5 has been taken out? What extra information has been included?

A famous person that I really admire is the professional snowboarder and skateboarder Shaun White. Shaun was born in San Diego, California on the September 3rd 1986 and by the age of six he was already snowboarding. He started competing when he was thirteen and turned professional when he was seventeen. Although he is still very young he has already won many gold medals in the X-games. In 2006 he won a gold medal in the halfpipe event at the Turin winter Olympics. I'm sure he will win many more. I'm a big fan of Shaun because I love extreme sports and he shows us exactly what a young person can do. He's amazing.

9 Now turn your profile from Exercise 6 into a short text.

Sounds right Questions

10 Questions you might want to use for interviews with famous people beginning with Wh-words (when, where, what) often have the following stress pattern OooO. Write three more questions and practise saying them.

O	o	o	o	o	o	o	o	o	O
Where	do	you	get	the	ideas	for	your	songs	from?
What	was	life	like	for	you	as	a		teenager?

UNIT 9

The city of Vancouver

Key words

| quality of life | current | community | climate |
| rainfall | scenery | temperate | minority |

1 Read the text. Would you like to go to Vancouver? Why or why not?

Vancouver is a city in the southwest of British Columbia, very close to the border with the USA, and it is the third largest in Canada (after Toronto and Montreal). The population in Greater Vancouver is just over 2 million people. It is named after a British explorer, Captain George Vancouver.

Vancouver is notable for several things. It is the third largest film production centre in North America (after Los Angeles and New York City). It is also a city with a good quality of life — in 2007, Vancouver was equal to Vienna as having the third highest quality of living in the world, after Zurich and Geneva.

It is a popular place for tourists, too, due mostly to its geography. Vancouver is set on the coast between the Strait of Georgia and the North Shore Mountains.

The city is famous for its beautiful scenery, and it has one of the largest city parks in North America, called Stanley Park. The North Shore Mountains can be seen from many places within the city, and on a clear day the views include: Mount Baker (the snow-capped volcano in the State of Washington, USA) to the southeast, Vancouver Island across the Strait of Georgia to the west and southwest, and the Sunshine Coast to the northwest. Vancouver also has beaches that are popular with residents and tourists during the summer. The mountains also offer skiing (nearby Whistler hosts the Winter Olympic Games in 2010).

Vancouver's climate is very temperate by Canadian standards, due to the warm ocean current that flows past the city. The summer months are sunny with moderate temperatures (the daily maximum averages 22°C in July and August) and are often quite dry as well. In contrast, more than half of all winter days receive measurable rainfall. On average, snow falls on only eleven days per year, with only three days receiving six centimetres or more.

2 Do the quiz.

1 Which are the two official languages of Canada?
   a) English and French   b) English and Spanish   c) English and Chinese
2 Which two languages are most spoken in Vancouver?
   a) English and French   b) English and Spanish   c) English and Chinese
3 What percentage of Vancouver's population is white?
   a) 51%   b) 71%   c) 75%
4 What are the two largest minority groups in Vancouver?
   a) Chinese and French   b) Chinese and Indian   c) Indian and Vietnamese

3 Read the text and check your answers.

Hongcouver

Many people know that Canada has two official languages, which are English and French. This is why the information on anything you buy in Canada is written in both languages. But not many people know that in Vancouver, the two main languages you'll hear in the streets are English and Mandarin Chinese.

The Chinese community in Vancouver is very large indeed – Mandarin Chinese is spoken as the first language in about 30% of the homes in Vancouver. There has been a Chinese community in British Columbia for a very long time, but it grew a great deal when many people came from Hong Kong (in the 1980s). The Chinese community is now so large that many people call the city 'Hongcouver'.

But the Chinese are not the only non-white community in Vancouver. Indeed, the white population makes up only 51% of the city's residents. The largest group after the Chinese are the Indians from SE Asia, but there are also significant numbers of people from countries such as Vietnam and Korea.

Mini-project City Guide

4 Choose a city that you know something about and/or are interested in. It could be a city in your own country, or somewhere else in the world. Research on the internet and find information about things like:

- its location
- its geographical features (e.g. is it on a river? is it near the sea or mountains?)
- its climate
- its population (ethnic mix)
- the language(s) that people speak

5 Write a text about the city you have chosen. Find/Download some photographs that can illustrate the main points of your text.

UNIT 9

UNIT 10 Crazy collectors

1 Look at the photo and the text. What does the man collect? When did he start? Read the text and check your answers.

Mister Sandman

When he goes on holiday, Nick D'Errico isn't interested in the sun and the sea. His only interest is ... sand! We asked him when his fascination with sand started.

Many years ago. My wife and I were on a holiday in Jamaica, on our honeymoon. One day we were on the beach. The sand was really beautiful and my wife asked me if we could take some of it home. She thought it would be a nice souvenir. I wasn't thinking of starting a new hobby, but I've been collecting sand since that holiday.

How did the hobby start?

Friends started bringing me sand from lots of exotic countries. When I looked at the sand through a microscope, I saw that there were lots of different kinds. I was fascinated, and that's how the hobby started. Now it takes up most of my free time.

Have you collected every type of sand?

Well, I don't know how many types of sand there are in the world! But I've collected between 18,000 and 19,000 different types. Last year a geology professor in North Carolina asked me if I wanted his collection. Of course, I said 'Yes'! His collection weighs 2,722 kilos. It's still in the packages it arrived in – it's taken over my house!

Do you know what the most expensive sand in the world is?

Probably moon sand. Not long ago some moon sand was stolen. It hasn't appeared on the black market yet. But when it does, it will be very, very expensive!

Can you tell me how to start if I want to become a sand collector?

Just go to the beach and stand there. Take your time and look closely. Take sand from different places on the beach. When you see how different all the kinds of sand are, your fascination will start.

How many members has the Sand Society got?

It started with six people. But it's been growing all the time for almost 40 years. 240 people have joined, from fourteen different countries.

In this unit

You learn
- present perfect continuous
- embedded questions
- words for hobbies and pastimes

and then you can
- talk about collecting something
- talk about hobbies

2 Circle the correct word in each sentence.

1 Nick collects *sand/DVDs*.
2 Nick and his wife were on honeymoon in *Hawaii/Jamaica*.
3 Nick's friends brought him sand from different *countries/cities*.
4 Nick has collected more than *18,000/19,000* types of sand.
5 He has a sand collection that his *wife/a professor* gave him.
6 The collection is still in boxes in *his house/in North Carolina*.
7 The most expensive sand is probably *moon sand/black sand*.
8 The Sand Society has members from *14/240* different countries.

Get talking Talking about collecting something

3 Listen and act out the dialogue.

A What's your hobby?
B Collecting stamps.
A How long have you been collecting them?
B Since 2002.
A How many have you got?
B About 600.
A Wow! That's a lot.

4 Play a game with a partner. Choose one of the people. Make dialogues to find out who your partner is thinking of.

A I'm thinking of a girl.
B What's her hobby?
A Collecting bags of sugar.
B How long has she been collecting them?
A For 8 months.
B How many has she got?
A About 300.
B It's Anne Marie.
A That's right.

Note:
Remember the use of *for* and *since*:
for 4 weeks / 2 months / 3 years
since my last birthday / August / 2004

Alan	Ken	Caroline	Barbara	Karen	Stewart
stamps	football pictures	sugar bags	shells	stamps	model planes
3 years	a year	2 years	last holiday	3 years	a long time
about 800	about 130	about 550	about 60	about 1.200	about 130

Anne Marie	**Rick**	**Jonathan**	**Nick**	**Chris**	**Carl**
bags of sugar	comics	shells	stamps	model planes	bags of sugar
8 months	half a year	2 years	3 years	a few months	2 months
about 300	about 40	about 100	about 200	about 60	about 100

Brenda	**Claudia**	**Lisa**	**Sue**	**Simon**	**Claire**
shells	football pictures	comics	comics	football pictures	model planes
last summer	6 months	last year	many years	3 years	2 years
about 120	about 200	about 70	about 450	about 200	about 90

5 Work with a partner. Act out similar dialogues about yourselves.

UNIT 10   95

Language Focus

Vocabulary Hobbies and pastimes

13 1 Match the activity to the correct photo. Then listen and check.

doing puzzles ☐	going bird-watching ☐	mending things ☐
doing photography ☐	keeping a blog ☐	doing pottery ☐
making models ☐	collecting things ☐	playing online games ☐

Get talking Talking about hobbies

2 Work with a partner. Ask and answer questions about hobbies.

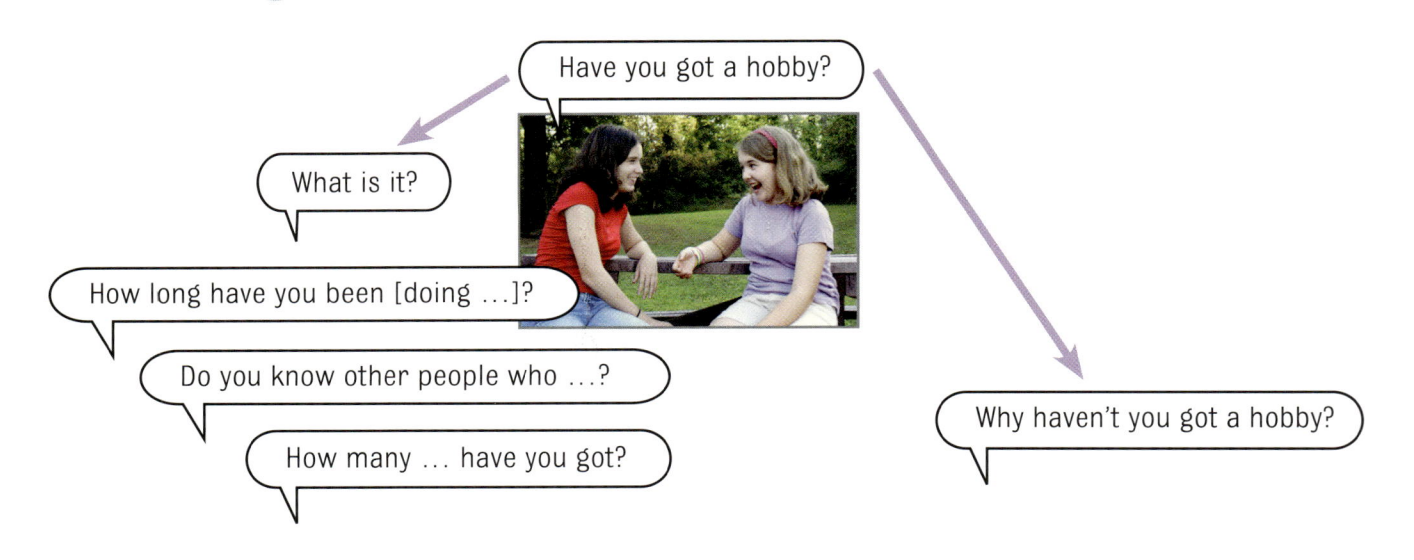

Have you got a hobby?

What is it?

How long have you been [doing …]?

Do you know other people who …?

How many … have you got?

Why haven't you got a hobby?

96 UNIT 10

Grammar

Present perfect continuous

1 Put the words in order to make the sentences. Check with the text on page 94.

collecting / since / sand / holiday. / been / that / I've /

almost / 40 years. / been / for / The Sand Society / growing / has /

Use the Present perfect progressive to talk about situations that started in the past and are still going on now. You also use it to stress how long an activity has been going on.

This is how you form the **present perfect continuous**:
Person + **have (has)** + **(n't)** + **been** + **ing** form of verb

He**'s been playing** football for 2 hours.
He **hasn't been studying** for a week.

This is how you form questions:
(Question word) + **have** + **person** + **been** + **ing** form of verb
What **have** you **been doing**?
How long **have you been collecting** shells?

2 Write sentences to answer the questions.

A (collect / 6 years)
Why has he got so many CDs?
He's been collecting CDs for 6 years.

B (eat ice-cream / an hour)
Why is she feeling sick?
....

C (lie in the sun / 6 hours)
Why is he sunburnt?
....

D (wait for the bus / 4 o'clock)
Why is she angry?
....
....

E (study / all morning)
Why is she tired?
....
....

F (ride his bike / all day)
Why is he thirsty?
....
....

3 Write sentences using the Present perfect continuous.

1 running around / the / garden / in / been / all morning. / They've / ....
2 playing / have / in a band? / you / been / How long / ....
3 hours. / to phone / for / We've / her / trying / been ....
4 been / London / years. / They've / living / 12 / in / for ....

UNIT 10   97

Embedded questions

4 **Which sentence is correct? Check on page 94 if necessary.**

a) I don't know how many types of sand there are in the world.
b) I don't know how many types of sand are there in the world.

Embedded questions are questions that are hidden in a sentence.
They often begin with *I don't know ……, Nobody knows ……, I have no idea. ……* etc.

5 **Read the embedded questions (1–4). Match them to the correct question (a–d).**

1 I don't know when the shop opens.
2 Nobody can tell me how much this costs.
3 I'm not sure how many CDs I've got.
4 Nobody knows when he'll be back.

a) How many CDs have you got?
b) When will he be back?
c) How much does this cost?
d) When does the shop open?

We'll never find out where the gorilla's hiding.

This is how you form embedded questions:
Question: Where has he gone?
Embedded question: I've no idea *where he's gone*.
Question: How old is it?
Embedded question: Nobody knows *how old it is*.

6 **Complete the answers.**

1 'What's her name?' 'Sorry – I don't know *who she is.* '
2 'Where does he live?' 'Sorry – I don't know ……………………'
3 'When did they arrive?' 'Sorry – I don't know ……………………'
4 'Where has he gone?' 'Sorry – I don't know ……………………'
5 'What's the time?' 'Sorry – I don't know ……………………'

7 **Write one sentence with an embedded question for each pair of sentences.**

1 What would you like to eat? I'm not sure. *I'm not sure what I'd like to eat.*
2 How old is she? I've got no idea.
3 Where did he go? Nobody knows.
4 Is it cold outside? We need to check.
5 Did she phone? I don't know
6 When does the film start? I'm not sure.

Skills

Listening

1 Listen to the conversation. Paul is asking about Monica's collection. Tick (✓) the things Monica collects.

2 Listen to the conversation again. Then circle the correct answer.

1 Monica started her collection *exactly / about* six years ago.
2 She was on a *driving / cycling* holiday with her parents in Spain.
3 She took the pens home *as presents for her friends / to start a collection*.
4 Now Monica has got *two thousand / five hundred and fifty pens* in her collection.
5 Monica's *parents / friends and their parents* bring pens back for her from their holidays.
6 Pens are easy to bring back because they're *cheap / light*.
7 Her favourite pen is from an expensive hotel in *Paris / San Francisco*.
8 Her favourite pen is made of *aluminium / plastic*.

Reading

3 Read the texts and answer these questions.

1 When did each of these people start collecting?
2 How many things have they collected so far?
3 When and why did they start their collections?

Marcela T. is 30 and works as a photographer in Buenos Aires, Argentina. She certainly has an unusual hobby: she collects tea bags. She started her hobby five years ago when she was on holiday in England with her husband. They were sitting in a tea shop and had ordered some tea. The waiter brought a pot of hot water and a wooden box with lots of different tea bags. Marcela, who had never really looked at tea bags before, began to study them carefully. She saw how colourful and attractive they were. So she asked friends to bring tea bags back from their holidays. So far, Marcela has collected over 5,000 tea bags from 49 different countries. 'Hopefully, my collection will keep on growing,' she says.

John M. is 26, and he has a rather unusual hobby. He collects bathroom taps. He started collecting them after his 20th birthday, when he was working as a plumber. He saw the bathrooms in many different houses, and found it interesting how many different kinds of taps people had. So one day he started collecting them, and so far he has collected over 600.
'Unfortunately, when my collection really started growing, there wasn't enough space in my house to keep all of them,' says John, 'so I rented an old factory to keep them in.' The factory is near his hometown, Portsmouth, in the south of England.
John's friends think he is crazy; naturally, John doesn't really agree. He just thinks he has an interesting hobby!

4 **Who is each sentence about – Marcela or John? Circle the correct name.**

1 *Marcela / John* started collecting six years ago.
2 *Marcela / John* gets help from friends.
3 *Marcela / John* started collecting while working.
4 *Marcela / John* started collecting during a holiday.
5 *Marcela / John* doesn't keep the collection at home.

5 **Circle T (True) or F (False) for the sentences below.**

1 Marcela started collecting tea bags at home. T / F
2 Marcela started collecting the bags because she liked the colours. T / F
3 Marcela wants her collection to get bigger. T / F
4 John received a bathroom tap as a present on his birthday. T / F
5 John has never kept the bathroom taps in his house. T / F
6 John doesn't think his hobby is crazy. T / F

Speaking

6 **Which collection is more/less interesting, Marcela's or John's? Why?**

7 **Interview three classmates about collecting things.**

Have you ever collected anything?
What was it?
When did you collect ….. ?

How long have you had your collection of … ?
How long did you collect …. ?
How many …. did you collect?
Have you still got any ….?

8 **Report to the class.**

I interviewed three classmates. One collected … when she was …
She still has got …
One collects … He has collected … since/for …
He's got …
One has never collected anything.

Writing

9 **Write a text about an unusual collector.**

- Search the internet for collectors of unusual things.
- Write a text of about 150 words about a real collector. Write another one about a collector that you invent.
- When you have finished, work in small groups. Do not tell each other which of your texts is about an imagined collector, and which is about a real one.
- Read all the texts in the group, and talk about which of the people you think are real and which are imagined.

Check your progress Units 9 and 10

1 Complete the words.

1 m_ _ _ solo artist
2 number 1 s_ _ _ _ _
3 f_ _ _ _ _ solo artist
4 number 1 a_ _ _ _

☐ 4

2 Reorder the letters and write the words.

1 doing **zusplez** ......
2 doing **typetor** ......
3 making **seldom** ......
4 playing **linnoe** games ......
5 **ginndem** things ......
6 keeping a **glob** ......
7 **gnectilloc** things ......
8 doing **groothhappy** ......

☐ 8

3 Complete the dialogue.

Max Who's your ¹............ singer?
Zoë I don't know. Maybe Enrique Iglesias.
Max Don't you like George Michael any ²............ ?
Zoë No, not really. I ³............ to like him, didn't I?
Max You were mad about him! How long have you ⁴............ listening to Enrique Iglesias?
Zoë About a year.
Max How many of his albums ⁵............ you got?
Zoë Only three.

☐ 5

4 Complete with *used to* and the words in brackets.

1 We .... live in Rome. (live)
2 Pablo .... jazz, but he does now. (not / like)
3 What .... to when you were 10? (you / listen)
4 .... long hair? (your brother / have)
5 Do you remember what .... you when you were a baby? (your parents / call).

☐ 5

5 Complete the sentences with the words below.

to seeing	on paying	at remembering
into playing	of going	on starting
in joining	of going	

1 Ken's fond .... to live concerts.
2 I'm really looking forward .... them live.
3 I'm keen .... a collection of CDs.
4 Don always insists .... for the meal.
5 Are you interested .... our band?
6 I'm hopeless .... people's birthdays.
7 We're thinking .... for a pizza. Want to come?
8 Help! My brother's .... loud music!

☐ 8

6 Rewrite the sentences using the Present perfect continuous and *for/since*.

1 Vicky started collecting clothes in 2004.
....
2 I only started listening to them last week.
....
3 He started making records 30 years ago.
....
4 I started downloading it this morning.
....
5 I started speaking Chinese four years ago.
....
6 They started playing the match yesterday.
....

☐ 12

7 Write embedded questions.

1 What's their fan club called?
I don't know ....
2 Where can I find out more about this hobby?
I'm not sure ....
3 What did he die of?
Nobody knows ....
4 When's the new album coming out?
Can you ask your brother ....
....

☐ 8

TOTAL ☐ 50

My progress so far is …

brilliant! ☐   quite good. ☐   not great. ☐

UNIT 10 101

Unusual collections

1 Read the text and decide if the sentences below are T (True) or F (False).

An unusual collection

On a family holiday at the age of eight, Joanne Browne was playing on the beach when she found a strange-looking stone. It was the first of a collection which now numbers over 2,000 items.

In the beginning, Joanne chose to collect stones because of their shape or colour. 'Anything that was nice or unusual, really,' she says 'Some of my friends were collecting stamps, which I thought was boring. I like collecting stones because it's something that gets me out of the house. And now that I have learned a little about geology, I find my collection even more fascinating. It's really interesting to discover why they are different, where they came from, how they were formed, and that sort of thing. I might even become a geologist one day'.

Lately, she's added some crystals and fossils to her collection. She says that her crystals can be found in many places but 'are worth more to me than diamonds, and just as beautiful'. Fossils, she says, are a new passion, 'I love the idea that I'm holding millions of years of history in my hand.' With the help of books and the Internet, Joanne now plans her holidays based on where she might find something unusual. 'It's not so much left to chance now, but that doesn't mean I won't pick up a stone and put it in my pocket just because it's nice!'

1. Joanne had 2,000 stones by the time she was eight. T/F
2. The first stones she collected were strange or attractive ones. T/F
3. She used to collect stamps before she started her collection of stones. T/F
4. She has made a career out of her hobby. T/F
5. Her crystals are worth a lot of money. T/F
6. Joanne's holidays are spent looking for things to add to her collection. T/F

Do you know?

The first steam train was built in 1804 in Wales. It carried 10 tons of iron, 70 men and 5 extra wagons. It travelled 9 miles and the journey took 2 hours.

2 Listen and then answer the questions about trainspotters.

1. Where can you find trainspotters?
2. What do they collect?
3. Why is Clapham Junction popular with trainspotters?
4. What do you need to be a trainspotter?
5. How do trainspotters communicate with each other?
6. Have you ever been on or seen any famous trains such as the Orient Express?

3 **Over 2 U!** In groups, discuss things you collect, or would like to collect.

MORE! And now you can watch *School Reporters!*

The day Britain's biggest egg collector climbed his last tree

Man falls to his death from tree while checking out unusual nest

Colin Watson's hobby was illegal, because since 1954 it has been against the law to take the eggs of wild birds. On a windy afternoon this week, Colin Watson risked too much. While a friend watched in horror, Watson, 63, fell out of a 12-metre tree he had climbed to check out the nest of a rare bird. The ambulance arrived soon afterwards, but the father of three died at the scene from his injuries.

It was the end of a life which saw a schoolboy hobby develop into a passion that made Watson the most notorious collector of wild birds' eggs in Britain for two decades. As a boy, Watson was fascinated by the beauty of bird's eggs and the fact that very rare birds like peregrines and goshawks nested near where he lived.

In those days egg collecting was not illegal. He grew up in a town called Selby, and some of his older neighbours were experienced egg collectors.

An RSPB inspector with illegally collected eggs.

They showed the boy how to blow eggs – to remove their contents through tiny holes. They also showed him how to start a collection.

Later, Watson became the biggest collector of wild birds' eggs in Britain. He was arrested many times for breaking the law, and the police fined him thousands of pounds. Some years ago, officers of the RSPB (The Royal Society for the Protection of Birds) went to Watson's house to search for his collection. They were shocked when they found more than 2,000 eggs, among them eggs of the very rare golden eagle.

'This is a very tragic incident,' said Graham Madge of the RSPB yesterday. 'It is very sad that Mr Watson's life ended like this, but what he did to the birds was also a tragedy.'

golden eagle    *goshawk*    *peregrine*    *bird's eggs in a nest*

For **MORE!** Go to www.cambridge.org/elt/more and do a quiz on this text.

UNIT 10

UNIT 11 Speak out

In this unit

You learn
- reported speech
- reported questions
- adjectives for personality

and then you can
- check what people do / explain what you do
- describe people

1 Listen and read.

Interviewer So Emily. You're a journalist in your free time, aren't you?

Emily Yes, that's right. I do interviews for Children's Express. It's an online magazine written by young people.

Interviewer Tell me more.

Emily Well, basically any young person can write a story and send it in. Last year more than 500 kids did something for the magazine.

Interviewer And what do you do for it?

Emily Well my favourite thing is doing interviews. For example, a month ago I did an interview with two brave teenagers from Manchester who are trying to stop animal testing by a local cosmetics company. I asked them what they thought they could do about it and they told me that they had organised a big demonstration outside the laboratories a few weeks ago. They're very patient because they know it will take a long time but they are also very determined and they said they would definitely continue to do all they can to stop it.

Interviewer So do you always do political stories?

Emily Oh no. I do all sorts. Only last week I talked to a 14-year-old boy who has to look after his sick mother as a carer. He told me that his life was hard but he said that he could see a light at the end of the tunnel. He was very positive. It was a very inspirational story for our readers.

Interviewer So how do you choose the stories you want to do?

Emily I like stories that have a message. I want young people to be more tolerant. I want them to think about how good their lives are. That's why I do the interviews.

2 Circle the correct word to complete the sentences.

1 Emily works as a journalist for a *newspaper/magazine*.
2 You can find Children's Express *in newsagent's/on the Internet*.
3 Emily did an interview with two *12/18*-year-old protesters.
4 Emily prefers doing stories about *politics/lots of different topics*.
5 Last week she talked to a boy who cares for his *brother/mother*.
6 The boy was feeling *good/bad* about the future.
7 Emily wants her readers to *accept/be more patient* with other people.

Get talking Checking what people do / explaining what you do

3 Match the dialogues with the correct pictures. Then listen and repeat.

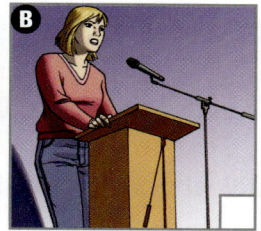

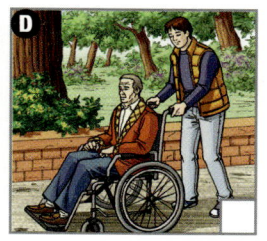

1 **Boy** You're a good artist aren't you?
  Girl Well, I like to do a bit of painting when I have time.

2 **Girl** You're a volunteer worker, aren't you?
  Boy That's right. I help at an old people's home on Saturdays.

3 **Girl** You're in a band, aren't you?
  Boy Yes, I play the drums.

4 **Boy** You're good at public speaking, aren't you?
  Girl I'm alright. I'm a member of the debating club.

4 Work with a partner. Use the prompts to make similar dialogues.

1 a good cook? – help mother in the kitchen
2 Liverpool fan? – watch games on TV
3 an animal lover? – have got three dogs, two cats
4 good at English? – get 98% in last test
5 a long-distance runner – do the London marathon last week
6 poet – write poems sometimes

Language Focus

Vocabulary Personality adjectives

1 Match the sentences with their endings.

1 Tony doesn't judge other people. He accepts everyone. He's …
2 Brian's not scared of anything. He's very …
3 Adriana loves doing new things. She's …
4 Simon always does the right thing to do. He's very …
5 Carl thinks about other people. He's …
6 Sharon doesn't like being the centre of attention. She's a bit …
7 Susie often shows how she is feeling. She's quite …
8 Poppy always sees the good in everything. She's so …

a) considerate
b) tolerant
c) positive
d) brave
e) adventurous
f) sensible
g) sensitive
h) shy

scared
negative
intolerant
unadventurous
insensitive
outgoing
silly
selfish

2 Now say the opposites of the adjectives. Choose from the words on the left.

3 Read the story. Use adjectives to describe Bob, Lucy, Jessica, Kevin and Cyril.

When the plane crashed into the sea, the survivors were lucky. There was a small island very near them and they all swam there. Bob wanted to get rescued immediately. He ran into the forest to get wood to start a fire. Nobody saw him again.
After that Cyril didn't want to go anywhere. He just sat on the beach shouting 'We're all going to die!' He didn't want to listen to anyone else's plans.
Jessica wanted to explore every part of the island to see what food she could find. She was sure they could find lots of things to eat. She quickly made friends with the others and organised a hunting party. Kevin tried to cheer other people up by saying that everything would be alright. Lucy didn't say anything to anyone. She just waited for a good signal and then called the rescue services on her mobile phone.

A I think Bob is impatient because he didn't wait.

B Yes, and he is stupid because he went into the jungle.

Get talking Describing people

4 Put the dialogue in order. Then listen and repeat.

….. **A** Why do you say that?
….. **A** Have you got a sister?
….. **A** What's she like?
….. **B** She waits for hours when I'm in the bathroom and she never complains.
….. **B** Yes I have. She's called Helen.
….. **B** She's a bit shy but she's very tolerant.

Grammar

Reported speech

1 Complete the table. Use the dialogue on page 104.

Direct speech	Reported speech
"My life is hard."	He told me that [1]....... life [2]....... hard
"We organised a big demonstration."	They told me [3]....... .... a big demonstration.
"We will do all we can to stop it."	They said [4]....... .... do all they can to stop it.
"I can see a light at the end of the tunnel."	He said that [5]....... .... see a light at the end of the tunnel.

Rules

When we want to report what someone has said, we commonly use the verbs *say* and *tell*. Notice the different ways we use them.
He said (that)...
He told me (that)... (With *tell* we use an object)

We also often change the tense used in the original sentence.
present simple ➔ past simple
present continuous ➔ past continuous
past/present perfect ➔ past perfect

will ➔ would
can ➔ could
is/are going to ➔ was/were going to

Remember to change the pronouns if necessary.

2 Here are some of the things one of the teenagers from Manchester told Emily. Change the reported speech back into the words that they said.

1 He said that he was really angry. *I'm really angry.*
2 He told me he was going to write a letter to the Prime Minister. .....
3 He said he would fight until the laboratory was closed. .....
4 He told me that they loved animals. .....
5 He said that they had a lot of support from the local people. .....
6 He told me they were organising another demonstration. .....
7 He told me that he had spent a lot of time on this case. .....
8 He said that they hadn't heard anything from the company yet. .....

3 Here are some more things that Emily told the interviewer. Report them using the verb in brackets.

1 I work for an on-line magazine. (say)
She said that she worked for an on-line magazine.

2 I'm just finishing my latest story. (tell)

3 I've met a lot of famous people. (say)

4 I interviewed George Clooney last year. (tell)

5 I'm going to interview Madonna soon. (say)

6 I'll send you a copy of my interview. (tell)

7 I can show you where I work. (said)

8 I was very happy with my last story. (tell)

UNIT 11 107

Reported questions

4 **Look at the examples of reported questions.**

1 I asked them why they were here   2 I asked them if that would be dangerous

Put the words in order to make the original questions.

a) it / dangerous / be / will / ?   b) are / ? / why / here / you

When we report questions, we use the verb 'ask someone (if/whether)' or 'wonder' or 'want to know'.
If the question has a question word like 'when/how/why/who/what/where' in it, we use the same question word in the reported question.
If the question is a 'Yes/No' question (= it *doesn't* have a question word) we use the word 'if' in the reported question.
We *don't* use auxiliaries like 'do/does' in reported questions – the word order is like a statement, not a question. (e.g. He asked me what I wanted – **not** He asked me ~~what did I want~~)
The tense of the verb in the question usually changes

5 **Write the original questions.**

1 He asked me what my name was. *What's your name?*
2 He asked me if I was Spanish. ....
3 He asked why I wanted to study English. ....
4 He asked me if I had studied English at school. ....
5 He asked me if I had visited the UK before. ....
6 He asked me how long I was going to stay in the UK. ....

6 **Put the words in the correct order.**

1 asked / My father / if / me / I / the answer / knew *My father asked me if I knew the answer.*
2 hungry / She / if / was / I / asked / me ....
3 asked / her / if / Steve / wanted / an ice cream / she ....
4 We / where / asked / her / she / bought / her shoes / had ....
5 I / what / her telephone number / asked / was / her ....
6 film / him / if / She / before / asked / seen / had / the ....
7 I / where / him / was / going / he / asked ....
8 her / if / He / asked / some / she / help / homework / with / her / wanted ....

7 **Complete the reported questions.**

1 'How old are you?'   She asked me *how old* I was.
2 'Where do you live?'   They asked me .... I lived.
3 'Where did you buy them?'   I asked her .... had bought them.
4 'Do you want to come with us?'   We asked him .... to come with us.
5 'Are you American?'   They asked me ....
6 'Have you ever been to Greece?'   He asked me ....
7 'When did you leave school?'   He asked her ....
8 'Who bought you the flowers'   He asked me ....

108 UNIT 11

Skills

Reading

1 Read Joanne's poem and choose the best title for it from the titles below.

| Fitting in | No more tears | Me | Odd one out |

When I was at secondary school, I really wanted to fit in. But I never did. There were these two girls who made my life miserable. They told stories about me to the other kids, to their mums and even to the teachers. Everybody hated me and I cried myself to sleep nearly every night. Things got better when I went to another school when I was 15. I made wonderful friends there and now I'm happy. I wrote a poem about it. In fact, I write a lot of poetry. It helps me with any problems I have.

I had always been the odd one out
I had never belonged to a crowd
and I had never sat with the popular girls
during school lunches,
watching the others
looking at us.

I had always wanted the popular kids
to ask me to their parties,
to whisper with me during lunch break,
to share yesterday's stories
and tomorrow's plans.

It never happened.

Now after years of crying,
of being the odd one out,
I'm a different girl
because I'm the one
who speaks out.

I'm no longer the girl they can bully,
I'm no longer the odd one out,
I was lucky because I have met — me.

2 Read the poem again and decide if the sentences are T (True) or F (False).

1 The poet was bullied by three girls at school.   T / F
2 Other students spread lies about the poet.   T / F
3 The poet felt happier at her new school.   T / F
4 The poet writes because it helps her feel better.   T / F
5 She went to a lot of parties.   T / F
6 She felt like she didn't have anyone to share things with.   T / F
7 She became happier when the other girls accepted her.   T / F
8 The poet believes it's important to know yourself.   T / F

UNIT 11

Listening and speaking

3 Listen to Samir, Jonathan and Helen talking about their lives. Which of these things do they *not* mention?

☐ school ☐ football ☐ TV ☐ problems
☐ shopping ☐ fighting ☐ music ☐ friends

4 Listen again and tick (✓) the correct answers.

1 Jonathan thinks
  ☐ Boys are cleverer than girls.
  ☐ Boys and girls watch the same things on TV.
  ☐ The differences between boys and girls aren't really very big.

2 Helen thinks
  ☐ girls like to work things out.
  ☐ girls and boys aren't so different.
  ☐ girls smoke more than boys.

3 Helen thinks
  ☐ young people should appreciate how good their lives are.
  ☐ most young people have a lot of problems.
  ☐ wars are stupid.

4 Samir
  ☐ gets into a lot of fights.
  ☐ listens to music to calm down.
  ☐ never gets angry.

5 Jonathan
  ☐ thinks life is really hard for young people.
  ☐ thinks friends are really important.
  ☐ gets a bit depressed sometimes.

5 Here are some of the opinions expressed in the listening. How much do you agree with them? Give each a score from 0 (I disagree 100%) to 5 (I agree 100%).

1 Girls do better at school than boys. ☐
2 Girls are better at solving problems. ☐
3 Girls get into fights more often than boys. ☐
4 Girls make things more complicated than boys. ☐
5 Music is very important in youth culture. ☐
6 It's always good to share your problem with an older person. ☐

6 Work in small groups and compare your answers.

Sound right Reporting direct speech

7 Work in pairs. Listen and repeat then practise reporting what Samir, Jonathan and Helen said:

Jonathan said (pause) 'I don't think there are so many differences.' (pause) and he said (pause) 'Well, there are some things…

Notice how there is a short pause before and after the quotes. Also the voice is higher on the quotes.

Reading and writing

8 Read the letters to an agony aunt and match each one to a picture.

1

Dear Agony Aunt,
My younger sister wants to hang around with my friends, but they aren't very interested in her. She keeps giving them little presents, and she hangs around in front of their houses and waits for them in the mornings. I know that they laugh about her. I know that they want her to leave them alone. Should I tell her that everyone is laughing about her? Or should I just wait it out?
Yours, Katie

2

Dear Agony Aunt,
There is a teacher at my school who is making my life difficult. She is always picking on me. She tells me off for talking when I'm not. She gives me terrible marks for all my homework. She even sent me to see the headmaster the other day. I don't know why she is doing this. What can I do? I'm starting to hate going to school.
Yours, Larry

9 Read the replies from the Agony Aunt. Which letter do you think each one talks about (Katie's – or Larry's)? Write K or L.

1. You need to find out why she is treating you this way. ☐
2. Talk to your parents. Maybe they can talk to her. ☐
3. If you are a good friend, you have to tell her. ☐
4. Be sensitive. Your sister obviously thinks she's friends with your friends. ☐
5. Remember, one day you might need her help. ☐
6. Are you sure your behaviour is always perfect? ☐

10 Write a reply to one of the letters. Use the replies in Exercise 9 to help you.

UNIT 11

Understanding poetry

Key words

concrete poetry
rhyme
pattern

shape poem
alliteration
(un)stressed syllable

poetic device
rhythm

1 **Read about poetry.**

Poetry is art. Writing a poem is like painting a picture, but using words instead of colours. As there are different styles and kinds of paintings, poems are different too. There are some poems, for example, where the shape of how words are arranged somehow also expresses the content. They are called concrete or shape poems. Here is an example:

> A
> dark
> green giant
> is standing, silent
> as a deserted forest,
> in the corner of my lounge.
> A hundred
> brightly coloured
> baubles like sparkling
> fruit hang from spiky branches.
> And tinsel, like a great golden snake,
> wraps and curls itself around its body.
> But
> best
> of all
> are the presents
> piled around its
> burnished base.

Other types of poems use special techniques, often called 'poetic devices' to create certain effects in the reader's mind. The following poetic devices are frequently used.

a) Rhyme pays attention to the sounds in the end parts of the words (fine, mine, sign)

b) Alliteration - pays attention to the first part of the words, when e.g. the initial consonants of words are repeated (seven swans swimming swiftly)

c) Rhythm – pays attention to the way stressed and unstressed syllables follow one another, very much like the beat (rhythm) in a song.

2 **Read the following poems. First of all, make sure you understand them. Look up any words you don't understand in a dictionary. Then read them out to each other in pairs and discuss these questions:**
- Which of the two poems uses rhyme, with alliteration as poetic devices?
- Which of the two poems do you like better? Why?

Poem 1:

A fly and a flea flew up in a flue.
Said the fly to the flea, "What shall we do?"
"Let's fly," said the flea.
"Let's flee," said the fly.
So they fluttered and flew up a flaw in the flue.

Poem 2:

Night time

by Lee Bennet Hopkins

How do dreams know
when to creep
into my head
when I fall off
to sleep?

UNIT 11

3 **Bringing rhyme and rhythm together: limericks.**

The word limerick comes from a town in Ireland. A limerick is a short poem that follows a very strict poetic form. A limerick would not be a limerick if it didn't have humour in it and didn't follow clear rules for rhythm and rhyme.

Read the limerick, then answer the following questions:

(1) A clumsy young fellow named Tim
(2) was never informed how to swim.
(3) He fell off a dock
(4) and sank like a rock.
(5) And that was the end of him.

How many lines does a limerick have? Which lines in the limerick rhyme with each other?

Match the following patterns of rhythm to the lines of the poem above.

(a)   da DEE da da DEE
(b)   da DEE da da DEE da da DEE or
        da DEE da da DEE da DEE

Mini-project Analysing a poem

4 Find an English poem that you like. Look up all the words you don't understand. Analyse it and look for all the poetic devices used in the poem. Read your poem out to the class and give a short report on your analysis.

5 Alternatively, use the poem here.

Don't think rivers,
Don't think fountains,
Don't think mountain streams or creeks.
Don't think pools or ponds or oceans.
Don't think lakes and don't think leaks.
Don't think wells or wet or water.
Don't think showers.
Don't think springs.
Don't think moist or damp or rainy.
Don't think hurricanes or things
That drizzle, dribble, drip, drop, flood or flow,
When there's no bathroom – and you gotta go.

© Judith Viorst

UNIT 12 A fair world?

1 Listen and read.

Did you know?

Coffee is the most **popular** drink in the world.
52% of Americans drink coffee.
Australians drink **60%** more coffee than tea.
A coffee tree can produce up to **6 kilos** of coffee a year.
Brazil produces **a third** of the world's coffee.
Oil is the number 1 commodity that is bought and sold in the world. Coffee is **number 2**.

Juanita Carlos has a small coffee farm in the hills of Honduras. She gets up at daybreak, has breakfast, and then starts working in the fields. She works very hard, and goes to bed very late, but she has very little money — just enough to buy food and clothes for herself and for her two children. She also looks after her elderly mother. She hasn't got a car, and she hasn't got a TV. She would buy those things if she got more money for her coffee. Juanita listens to the radio every morning. She wants to hear what they say about the price of coffee in faraway New York. The news she hears is usually bad. Coffee prices are low and Juanita is very worried.

'If I had known that coffee prices would go down so much, I would have sold the farm a long time ago,' Juanita says. Where Juanita lives, all the small farmers and their families are as poor as she is.

Ramon Machado's farm is only three hours away from Juanita's. Ramon is not as worried as Juanita and he doesn't listen to the radio every morning to find out about coffee prices.

Ramon and twenty other farmers are part of a 'Fair Trade' project. They get a fixed price for their coffee. The project is not only about paying farmers a fair price for their products. Members of the Fair Trade project also refuse to use pesticides. On their small farms there are lots of trees that give shade to the coffee plants. Among them there are banana trees and avocado trees. This is good for the environment.

Ramon joined the project a year ago. Now he is happy because he doesn't have to worry about feeding his children or buying them clothes or books for school. If other farmers got a fixed price for their coffee too, their situation would be much better.

In this unit

You learn
- *If*-clauses (Revision)
- words for work places

and then you can
- talk about what you would have done
- talk about places

114 UNIT 12

2 Complete the sentences about Juanita and Ramon.

1 Juanita has a small .... in ....
2 She works very ...., but ....
3 She hasn't got a car or a ....
4 Every morning she listens to .... because she ....
5 Ramon is not as worried about .... as ....
6 Ramon doesn't listen ....
7 Ramon gets a fixed ....
8 Ramon is part of a ....

Get talking Talking about what you would have done

3 Read the dialogue. Write the correct names Alan, Paula, Liam or Grace under the person. Then listen and repeat.

1 .... 2 .... 3 .... 4 ....

Don   So I was walking down the street when this huge dog ran in front of me. I didn't know what to do.
Alan I'd have run away.
Paula I'd have thrown a stick for it.
Liam I'd have shouted at it.
Grace I'd have walked past it.

4 Work in groups of three. Take it in turns to describe the situation and say what you would have done. Use the prompts to help you.

1 The soup came and it was cold.
   send it back / not eat it

   A I'd have sent it back.
   B I wouldn't have eaten it.

2 I lent Joe my CD and he lost it.
   ask for a new one / tell him not to worry about it

3 I had a really important test but I hadn't studied.
   pretend to be ill / do it and hope for the best

4 I knocked on his door but he didn't answer.
   go home / call his mobile

UNIT 12   115

Language Focus

Vocabulary Work places

1 Match these people to the places where they work. Write the correct number in the box.

- [ ] a gym
- [ ] a hotel
- [ ] a mine
- [ ] a factory
- [ ] an office block
- [ ] a warehouse
- [ ] a laboratory
- [ ] a prison
- [ ] a court
- [ ] a farm

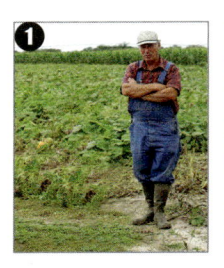

1. farmer
2. miner 
3. factory worker 
4. scientist 
5. judge 
6. office worker 
7. prison warden 
8. warehouse worker 
9. porter 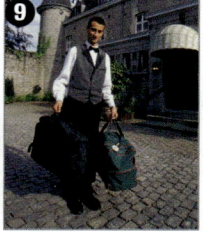
10. aerobics teacher 

2 Choose one of the workers in Exercise 1. Mime an action that person might do for the other students to guess.

You're milking a cow. You're on a farm.

Get talking Talking about places

3 Read the dialogues and complete them with the words on the left.

where
prison
criminals
factory

A What does your dad do?
B He's a warden. He works in a ¹............
A What's that?
B It's a place where ²............ go.

A What does your mum do?
B She's works in a ³............
A What's that?
B It's a place ⁴............ people make things.

4 Listen and check. Then practise the dialogues with a partner.

5 Use the prompts to make similar dialogues.

1. miner / mine / dig things out of the ground
2. work in a warehouse / store things before they go to the shops
3. scientist / laboratory / do experiments
4. aerobics teacher / gym / do exercise

116   UNIT 12

Grammar

If-clauses (Revision)

First conditional

Use the first conditional to talk about things that are in the future.
If-clause: If + subject + Present simple, **Main clause:** subject + **will/won't** + **infinitive**

1 **Match the sentence halves.**

1. If more farmers stop using pesticide
2. If more farmers join the Fair Trade projects
3. If you listen to the news …

a) you'll find out more about the situation.
b) it'll be good for the environment.
c) they won't have to worry about coffee prices.

Note: the **if** clause and main clause often change position.
The main clause can come before the If-clause.

2 **Complete the sentences with the correct form of the verbs in brackets.**

1. If you have time, I .... you my new computer. (show)
2. They'll get angry if they .... the news. (hear)
3. Mum .... you more pocket money, if you only buy sweets. (not give)
4. Our team .... the match if they carry on playing so well. (win)
5. If it is really his birthday on Monday, I .... him a nice present. (buy)
6. If he doesn't answer my emails, I .... to him again. (not write)

Second conditional

We use the Second conditional to talk about situations that we don't expect to happen or which are unreal.
If-clause: If + subject + Past simple, **Main Clause:** subject + **would ('d)/wouldn't** + **infinitive**
If Juanita got more money for her coffee, she would (she'd) buy a car.

3 **Which statement is correct?**

a) Juanita has a car because she is getting a better price for her coffee.
b) Juanita doesn't have the money to buy a car.

4 **Read out the sentences. Use the correct forms.**

1. If I *would have / had* more time, I *would go / went* to the cinema with you.
2. If all farmers *would hear / heard* about Fair Trade projects, it *would be / was* good.
3. *We'd help / We helped* you with your homework, if *we knew / would know* the answers.
4. If Peter *would play / played* tennis, he *was / would be* fitter.
5. She *were / would be* very angry, if she *heard / would hear* what you said.
6. If I *would be / were* you, *I'd work / I work* harder.

UNIT 12

5 Complete the sentences with the correct form of the verb in brackets.

1 What would you say if I .... you this camera as a present? (give)
2 I .... not .... that if I were you. (not do)
3 The computer .... a lot more expensive if you wanted the bigger hard disk. (be)
4 If I had her phone number, I'......................... it to you. (give)
5 If I .... £1,000, I'd buy a new mountain bike. (have)
6 They'd buy a bigger house if they .... the money. (have)

6 Read the sentences and say if they are first or second conditionals.

1 I'll buy it if I have enough money. ....
2 I'd buy it if I had enough money. ....
3 If you eat any more you'll be ill. ....
4 If you ate that you'd die. ....
5 If it's a new dress I'll be really happy. ....
6 If it was green it'd be perfect. ....

Second conditional /Questions

To ask a question using the Second conditional you simply reverse the word order.
You would buy Fair Trade products if there was a shop in your street.

Would you buy Fair Trade products if there was a shop in your street?

---

7 Match the questions and answers.

1 What would you buy if I gave you £500?
2 Would you help me if I asked you?
3 Where would you like to live?
4 Would Sarah come to the party?
5 How long would you need my bike?
6 Which film star would you like to meet?

a) Of course I would.
b) She would, if you invited her.
c) I'd bring it back tomorrow if you lent it to me.
d) Anywhere by the sea.
e) A new mobile phone.
f) Penelope Cruz. She does a lot to help poor people.

8 Put the words in order to make questions.

1 animal / what / like / you / be / would / to *What animal would you like to be?*
2 like / you / to / would / go / holidays / where / for / your ....
3 like / what / you / superpower / to / would / have ....
4 found / on / diamond / you / do / if / you / a / floor / would / ring / what / the ....
5 like / person / famous / most / what / would / you / to / meet ....
6 like / question / person / would / one / you / what / to / this / ask ....

9 Work with a partner. Ask the questions from Exercise 8. Take it in turns to answer each one.

A What animal would you like to be?

B I'd like to be a dolphin.

Skills

Listening

1 Look at the pictures. Number them in the correct order to tell a story. Then listen and check.

A   B   C

D   E   F

Reading

2 Read Jessica's diary entry about an unfair situation at school.

I'll never forget what happened to me today in my maths class. We had this new teacher, Mr Twaine. He's very young, and it was our first lesson with him. Nick wanted to make life difficult for him. Mr Twaine turned his back to us to write something on the board, and Nick started to make little balls of paper which he started to throw at the teacher! When the teacher turned round to check who it was, Nick stopped of course. This went on for some time, and the whole class started to laugh. I didn't think it was funny at all.

Anyway, Mr Twaine kept on talking, and he was still very friendly. When he turned his back to the class again, suddenly it happened. One of Nick's paper balls landed on my head. I was furious. I picked it up and threw it back at Nick. Suddenly Mr Twaine turned round, and saw me throwing the paper ball!

He looked at me for a long time, and then he said. 'Don't you think throwing paper balls is a bit childish? Stop it now and pick up all the balls from the floor.' He was pretty angry.

What should I have done? If I said it wasn't me, would the teacher believe me? After all he had seen me throw the paper. If I said it was Nick, Nick would be angry. I wouldn't like that. So I got up from my seat, and picked up all the paper balls from the floor. Nick was sitting there smiling. I thought that was really unfair!

3 Circle T (True) or F (False) for the sentences below.

1 The story happened two years ago in Jessica's maths class. T / F
2 It was Mr Twaine's first lesson with Jessica's class. T / F
3 Nobody found it funny when Nick threw little balls of paper. T / F
4 Jessica was furious because Nick hit her friend Sandra on her head. T / F
5 Mr Twaine said that throwing paper balls was for small children. T / F

UNIT 12

Speaking

4 Match the words to make phrases. Check your answers with a partner.

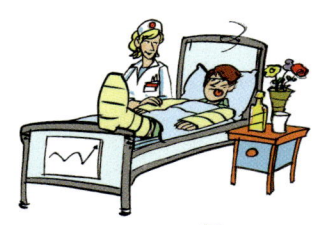

1 have   a) hospital
2 go to b) basketball
3 study c) food
4 fail   d) a crash
5 grow   e) prison
6 play   f) hard
7 steal g) a test
8 go to h) coffee

5 Read the situations. Do you think they are fair or unfair? Give your reasons.

a) A racing driver is in a very bad crash. He goes to hospital, where two nurses help him. The racing driver earns £15 million a year. The nurses each earn £12,000 a year.

b) A girl studies very hard for a test and gets a mark of 62%. Another girl doesn't study for the test at all, but gets 96% (without cheating).

c) A coffee farmer in Latin America grows coffee and sells it to a multinational coffee company for 25p a kilo. The company sells the coffee in the USA and Europe for £3.10 a kilo.

d) A school has a basketball team – for girls only. Boys can play on the basketball court in the school, but they can't be in the school team.

e) In a certain country, men and women always get the same pay if they do the same job. Men can stop working when they are 63; women can stop working when they are 60.

f) A man with no job steals some food from a shop – he goes to prison for 6 months. A rock star is caught when he steals a pair of trousers from a shop – he pays a fine of £10,000.

It's not fair if…..

I don't think it's fair when …..

That's completely unfair!

I don't think it's unfair at all.

Writing for your Portfolio

6 Think about something fair or unfair which happened. Write a diary entry about it.

120 UNIT 12

Check your progress Units 11 and 12

1 Complete the words to make adjectives.
1 consider_ _ _
2 _ _toler_ _ _
3 _ _adventur_ _ _
4 _ _sensit_ _ _
5 sensib_ _

[5]

2 Complete the names of the workplaces.
1 Where food is grown and animals are kept.
   f_ _ _ _
2 Where a judge works. c_ _ _ _
3 Underground where we find coal. m_ _ _
4 Where lots of things are stored.
   w_ _ _ _ _ _ _ _
5 Where scientists do experiments.
   l_ _ _ _ _ _ _ _ _

[5]

3 Say what you would do if the following happened to you.
1 A letter came to your house by mistake.
   ....
2 Your English teacher gave you a very low mark for your homework.
   ....
3 Somebody said you had stolen some money but you knew you hadn't.
   ....
4 Somebody helped you with a problem.
   ....

[8]

4 Rewrite in reported speech.
1 I'm going out.
   She said ....
2 I don't understand.
   He said ....
3 I was looking for you.
   He told me ....
4 I had an accident.
   She told me ....
5 I have seen this somewhere before.
   He said ....

[10]

5 Write the reported questions.
1 Where did you go?
   He ....
2 Do you want an ice cream?
   She ....
3 Do you think it will be expensive?
   He ....
4 How often do you watch the news on TV?
   She ....

[8]

6 Choose the correct answers.
1 If people *take / took* action now, we will stop the damage.
2 If we *score / scored* one more goal, we would win.
3 If George *will do / does* that again, I'll scream!
4 It *didn't / wouldn't* happen again if you were careful.
5 I *don't / won't* help you if you are impolite.
6 If I *had / have* money I would go to Spain.

[6]

7 Rewrite in the second conditional.
1 I'm not rich, so I can't buy you a car.
   If ....
2 I'm not interested, so I won't buy the DVD.
   If ....
3 He hasn't got any money so he can't go on holiday.
   If ....
4 He wants to join the army but he's not old enough.
   If ....

[8]

TOTAL [50]

My progress so far is ...

brilliant! ☐   quite good. ☐   not great. ☐

UNIT 12   121

Ethical buying!

1 Read the article about buying ethically. Then, work with a partner and discuss the questions below.

Buying ethically

You are out shopping with friends and you find a great new shirt. It's just what you're looking for and it's cheap. But what would you do if you found out that a six-year old child had made that shirt? Would you put it back or would you buy it anyway?

Buying ethically means that the things we pay for are not made by people who were paid almost nothing. It means not buying things that were made by children who should be at school. Buying ethically also means that the environment is not damaged in order to make the goods.

Despite this, in many countries around the world, young children are made to spend long days working for very low pay, sometimes far away from their families. There have been many stories of children – sometimes as young as six – being beaten for not working hard enough. There are also thousands of cases where the environment has been badly damaged by people who only care about money.

How can you help? Next time you are shopping, ask where things were made. There are several organisations which only buy and sell things which have been made using ethical standards. And if you don't think it's worth the effort, ask yourself if you would look good in a shirt that was made by an unhappy, terrified child, or a pair of shoes that were made using chemicals which destroyed that child's village.

1 What does buying ethically mean?
2 What happens when we don't buy ethically?
3 What happens to children who don't work hard?
4 What can we do to help the situation?
5 Why does the writer mention the shirt and shoes at the end?

Do you know?

Cotton is the world's dirtiest agricultural product. It releases more insecticides than any other crop in the world. The toxic chemicals sprayed on cotton crops pollute the land, air, food and drinking water and can cause health problems. Cotton is also the world's thirstiest crop.

2 The information below came from a survey in Britain. Guess the percentages and write (e.g. 70%) next to each item. Then listen and check your answers.

People who ...	Percentage
don't care how their clothes are produced.	....
would pay more for ethically-made clothes.	....
want to see an end to child labour.	....
care about damage to the environment.	....
ask about where clothes are made.	....
would like us to use fewer chemicals when making clothes.	....
care more about price than anything else.	....

3 **Over 2 U!** In groups write questions for an ethical shopping survey. As a class, choose the best questions. Then do the survey in class and with other classes.

MORE! And now you can watch *School Reporters!*

122 UNIT 12

Fair? Well...

(They are in a classroom, working. The bell rings for the end of the lesson)

Teacher OK, so that's it for today, you lot. But, of course, before you go, here's your homework for tonight …

James Oh, sir – no, please! That's not fair!

Teacher Really? How come?

Maggie You've given us homework twice already this week, sir.

Teacher You're right – I have. And?

James And there's the match tonight, sir. You know, the England game.

Teacher It's only a friendly, James – it's not a big match. And anyway, you've got time before it starts, haven't you?

James Yeah but I wanted some time to play my new Simpsons computer game.

Teacher So my homework's going to interrupt your evening's entertainment. I am sorry, James. Yes, Maggie. What is it?

Maggie Oh, please sir – don't give us homework tonight.

Teacher Why, Maggie? What are you doing that's so important? Don't tell me you want to watch the game too!

Maggie No way. But I've got loads of geography for Mr Newson for tomorrow.

Teacher So Mr Newson's allowed to give you homework but I'm not. That's not exactly fair either, is it? When did Mr Newson give you this homework, anyway?

Maggie Last Thursday.

Teacher So you've had nearly a week to do your homework and chosen to leave it all until the last minute. That's not exactly my fault, is it?

Maggie But sir, pleeeeease.

Teacher OK. Let's see. If I don't give you homework, you don't study enough. If you don't study enough, you don't pass the exams. If you don't pass the exams, your parents get angry and complain to the headmaster. And I get the headmaster complaining to me. And I lose my job. How fair is that?

James That's a bit over-dramatic, sir.

Teacher Well, James, that's because I went to drama school.

Maggie So, did you want to be an actor, sir?

Teacher Yes, I did, but we're not going to talk about that now because I'm going to give you your homework. OK?

James But sir, that's not …

Teacher … and if anyone says 'That's not fair', they'll get double homework.

James That's double unfair, sir.

Teacher Careful James! Now, let me think. OK, for homework, I want a 500 word essay with the title 'Why isn't life fair?'

Maggie *(ironically)* Oh, nice one, sir.

Teacher Thanks, Maggie. OK, give it to me in Friday's lesson. That's two days you've got. Bye everyone. Enjoy the match, James!

Read MORE for pleasure

For **MORE!** Go to www.cambridge.org/elt/more and do a quiz on this text.

Wordlist

Unit 1

batting gloves /ˈbætɪŋ ˌglʌvz/
beliefs /bɪˈliːfs/
bog /bɒg/
boots /buːts/
boxes /ˈbɒksɪz/
colony /ˈkɒləni/
conkers /ˈkɒŋkəz/
gloves /glʌvz/
goggles /ˈgɒglz/
harvest /ˈhɑːvɪst/
helmet /ˈhelmɪt/
hundreds of people /ˈhʌndrədz əv ˌpiːpl/
incredible /ɪnˈkredəbl/
muddy /ˈmʌdi/
pads /pædz/
pair of flippers /ˌpeər əv ˈflɪpəz/
port /pɔːt/
quarterback /ˈkwɔːtəbæk/
seeds /siːdz/
shorts /ʃɔːts/
snorkel /ˈsnɔːkl/
socks /sɒks/
steep hill /ˌstiːp ˈhɪl/
string /strɪŋ/
to be lucky /tə ˌbi ˈlʌki/
to belong /tə bɪˈlɒŋ/
to chase /tə ˈtʃeɪs/
to end up /tu ˌend ˈʌp/
to grow corn /tə ˌgrəʊ ˈkɔːn/
to pay taxes /tə ˌpeɪ ˈtæksɪz/
to roll /tə ˈrəʊl/
to take part /tə ˌteɪk ˈpɑːt/
trainers /treɪnɜːrs/
turkey /ˈtɜːki/
vest /vest/

Unit 2

bottom /ˈbɒtəm/
deepest /ˈdiːpɪst/
disgusting /dɪsˈgʌstɪŋ/
flight /flaɪt/
grade /greɪd/
height /haɪt/
millions /ˈmɪljənz/
plaque /plæk/
quiet /ˈkwaɪət/
rocket /ˈrɒkɪt/
scared /skeəd/
seat /siːt/
space shuttle /ˈspeɪs ˌʃʌtl/
sunrise /ˈsʌnraɪz/
sunset /ˈsʌnset/
to break up /tə ˌbreɪk ˈʌp/
to carry /tə ˈkæri/
to cause problems /tə ˌkɔːz ˈprɒbləmz/
to get into /tə ˌget ˈɪntu/
to land /tə ˈlænd/
to race /tə ˈreɪs/
to re-enter /tə riːˈentə(r)/
to risk /tə ˈrɪsk/
to run out of something /tə ˌrʌn ˈaʊt əv ˌ.../
to set off /tə ˌset ˈɒf/
to soak /tə ˈsəʊk/
to step /tə ˈstep/
to strike /tə ˈstraɪk/
top /tɒp/
vehicles /ˈviːəklz/
weird /wɪəd/

Unit 3

asteroid /ˈæstərɔɪd/
brand new /ˌbrænd ˈnjuː/
burning process /ˈbɜːnɪŋ ˌprəʊses/
challenge /ˈtʃælɪndʒ/
change /tʃeɪndʒ/
credit card /ˈkredɪt ˌkɑːd/
debit card /ˈdebɪt ˌkɑːd/
engine /ˈendʒɪn/
exhausted /ɪgˈzɔːstɪd/
fear /fɪə(r)/
fuel /ˈfjuːəl/
high pressure gas /ˌhaɪ ˌpreʃə ˈgæs/
hose /həʊz/
launch /lɔːntʃ/
leather /ˈleðə(r)/
lifestyle /ˈlaɪfstaɪl/
mass /mæs/
second-hand section /ˌsekənd ˈhænd ˌsekʃn/
temperature /ˈtemprətʃə(r)/
tiring /ˈtaɪərɪŋ/
to cut up /tə ˌkʌt ˈʌp/
to exchange /tu ɪksˈtʃeɪndʒ/
to load /tə ˈləʊd/
to solve a problem /tə ˌsɒlv ə ˈprɒbləm/
to suppose /tə səˈpəʊz/
to waste /tə ˈweɪst/
to weigh /tə ˈweɪ/
wages /ˈweɪdʒɪz/

Unit 4

a nap /ə ˈnæp/
a window cleaner /ə ˈwɪndəʊ ˌkliːnə(r)/
ambitious /æmˈbɪʃəs/
arrogant /ˈærəgənt/
creative /kriˈeɪtɪv/
customers /ˈkʌstəməz/
dishwasher /ˈdɪʃwɒʃə(r)/
easy-going /ˌiːzi ˈgəʊɪŋ/
efficient /ɪˈfɪʃnt/
friendly /ˈfrendli/
hard-working /ˌhɑːd ˈwɜːkɪŋ/
helpful /ˈhelpfl/
honest /ˈɒnɪst/
imaginative /ɪˈmædʒɪnətɪv/
independent /ˌɪndɪˈpendnt/
kind /kaɪnd/
ladder /ˈlædə(r)/
lunchtime rush /ˌlʌntʃtaɪm ˈrʌʃ/
morning shift /ˈmɔːnɪŋ ˌʃɪft/
patient /ˈpeɪʃnt/
peace keeping force /ˈpiːs ˌkiːpɪŋ ˌfɔːs/
polite /pəˈlaɪt/
prisoners /ˈprɪznəz/
ravens /ˈreɪvnz/
responsible /rɪˈspɒnsəbl/
soldier /ˈsəʊldʒə(r)/
the sight of /ðə ˈsaɪt əv/
to be haunted /tə ˌbi ˈhɔːntɪd/
to be successful /tə ˌbi səkˈsesfl/
to get ready /tə ˌget ˈredi/
to involve /tu ɪnˈvɒlv/
to land /tə ˈlænd/
to lock up /tə ˌlɒk ˈʌp/
to look after /tə ˌlʊk ˈɑːftə(r)/
to lose /tə ˈluːz/
to make jokes /tə ˌmeɪk ˈdʒəʊks/
to take a course /tə ˌteɪk ə ˈkɔːs/
to wait tables /tə ˌweɪt ˈteɪblz/
tower /ˈtaʊə(r)/
well-paid /ˌwel ˈpeɪd/

Unit 5

breeding grounds /ˈbriːdɪŋ ˌgraʊndz/
bright /braɪt/
confusing /kənˈfjuːzɪŋ/
creatures /ˈkriːtʃəz/
currents /ˈkʌrənts/
daylight /ˈdeɪlaɪt/
disappointed /ˌdɪsəˈpɔɪntɪd/
dream /driːm/
ending /ˈendɪŋ/
enemy /ˈenəmi/
eyesight /ˈaɪsaɪt/
have another go /ˌhæv əˌnʌðə ˈgəʊ/
parachute /ˈpærəʃuːt/
plankton /ˈplæŋktən/
predators /ˈpredətəz/
relative /ˈrelətɪv/
series /ˈsɪəriːz/
steam /stiːm/
thrilling /ˈθrɪlɪŋ/
to burn /tə ˈbɜːn/
to care about something /tə ˈkeər əbaʊt ˌ.../
to cram into something /tə ˈkræm ˌɪntə ˌ.../
to fall asleep /tə ˌfɔːl əˈsliːp/

to feed /tə ˈfiːd/
to give birth /tə ˌgɪv ˈbɜːθ/
to hang out /tə ˌhæŋ ˈaʊt/
to hurtle /tə ˈhɜːtl/
to insist /tu ɪnˈsɪst/
to jolt /tə ˈdʒɒlt/
to knock over something /tə ˈnɒk ˌəʊvə .../
to lay eggs /tə ˌleɪ ˈegz/
to migrate /tə maɪˈgreɪt/
to pick /tə ˈpɪk/
to put something down /tə ˌpʊt ... ˈdaʊn/
to recommend /tə rekəˈmend/
to run into someone /tə ˈrʌn ˌɪntə .../
to stand up /tə ˌstænd ˈʌp/
to take after someone /tə ˌteɪk ˈɑːftə .../
to take up something /tə ˌteɪk ˈʌp .../
to turn up the volume /tə ˌtɜːn ˌʌp ðə ˈvɒljuːm/
view /vjuː/
walk out /ˌwɔːk ˈaʊt/
waterfalls /ˈwɔːtəfɔːlz/

Unit 6

book fair /ˈbʊk ˌfeə(r)/
car show /ˈkɑː ˌʃəʊ/
cycling race /ˈsaɪklɪŋ ˌreɪs/
fashion show /ˈfæʃn ˌʃəʊ/
fireworks display /ˈfaɪəwɜːks dɪˌspleɪ/
front page /ˌfrʌnt ˈpeɪdʒ/
memories /ˈmeməriz/
opening night /ˈəʊpənɪŋ ˌnaɪt/
put up the tent /ˌpʊt ˌʌp ðə ˈtent/
rock festival /ˈrɒk ˌfestɪvl/
school fete /ˌskuːl ˈfeɪt/
strawberries /ˈstrɔːbriz/
tennis tournament /ˈtenɪs ˌtʊənəmənt/
to camp /tə ˈkæmp/
to draw /tə ˈdrɔː/

to get the chance /tə ˌget ðə ˈtʃɑːns/
to pick up /tə ˌpɪk ˈʌp/
to rent something /tə ˈrent .../
to stay overnight /tə ˌsteɪ əʊvəˈnaɪt/

Unit 7

artificial /ˌɑːtɪˈfɪʃl/
baked /beɪkt/
boiled /bɔɪld/
celery /ˈseləri/
cookery /ˈkʊkəri/
courgette /kɔːˈʒet/
curry /ˈkʌri/
fattening /ˈfætnɪŋ/
filling /ˈfɪlɪŋ/
fried /fraɪd/
grilled /grɪld/
growth /grəʊθ/
harmful /ˈhɑːmfl/
health /helθ/
healthy /ˈhelθi/
light /laɪt/
mild /maɪld/
minerals /ˈmɪnərəlz/
nutritious /njuːˈtrɪʃəs/
packets /ˈpækɪts/
popularity /ˌpɒpjəˈlærəti/
proteins /ˈprəʊtiːnz/
raw /rɔː/
revolting /rɪˈvəʊltɪŋ/
roast /rəʊst/
sickly /ˈsɪkli/
sound /saʊnd/
sour /ˈsaʊə(r)/
spicy /ˈspaɪsi/
starving /ˈstɑːvɪŋ/
sweet /swiːt/
to attract /tu əˈtrækt/
to decline /tə dɪˈklaɪn/
to define /tə dɪˈfaɪn/
to own something /tu ˈəʊn .../
to regret something /tə rɪˈgret .../
to run something /tə ˈrʌn .../
to taste /tə ˈteɪst/
vitamins /ˈvɪtəmɪnz/

Unit 8

amazed /əˈmeɪzd/
amazing /əˈmeɪzɪŋ/
ancient /ˈeɪnʃənt/
body piercing /ˈbɒdi ˌpɪəsɪŋ/
bridesmaid /ˈbraɪdzmeɪd/
clowns /klaʊnz/
courage /ˈkʌrɪdʒ/
demons /ˈdiːmənz/
disappointed /ˌdɪsəˈpɔɪntɪd/
disappointing /ˌdɪsəˈpɔɪntɪŋ/
distance /ˈdɪstəns/
earrings /ˈɪərɪŋz/
fascinated /ˈfæsɪneɪtɪd/
fascinating /ˈfæsɪneɪtɪŋ/
fashionable /ˈfæʃnəbl/
frightened /ˈfraɪtnd/
index finger /ˈɪndeks ˌfɪŋgə(r)/
insulting /ɪnˈsʌltɪŋ/
ornaments /ˈɔːnəmənts/
ritual /ˈrɪtʃuəl/
soles /səʊlz/
statue /ˈstætʃuː/
stockings /ˈstɒkɪŋz/
talents /ˈtælənts/
thumb /θʌm/
tiring /ˈtaɪərɪŋ/
to be polite /tə ˌbi pəˈlaɪt/
to be rude /tə ˌbi ˈruːd/
to cross your legs /tə ˌkrɒs jɔː ˈlegz/
to fold your arms /tə ˌfəʊld jɔːr ˈɑːmz/
to greet someone /tə ˈgriːt .../
to ignore someone /tu ɪgˈnɔː .../
to imitate /tu ˈɪmɪteɪt/
to insult /tu ɪnˈsʌlt/
to nod /tə ˈnɒd/
to point /tə ˈpɔɪnt/
to point a finger /tə ˌpɔɪnt ə ˈfɪŋgə(r)/
to scare someone /tə ˈskeə .../
to scratch your head /tə ˌskrætʃ jɔː ˈhed/
to shake hands /tə ˌʃeɪk ˈhændz/

to shake your head /tə ˌʃeɪk jɔː ˈhed/
to sigh /tə ˈsaɪ/
to sink /tə ˈsɪŋk/
to wave /tə ˈweɪv/
trendy /ˈtrendi/
unclean /ˌʌnˈkliːn/
worried /ˈwʌrid/
worrying /ˈwʌriɪŋ/

Unit 9

awards /əˈwɔːdz/
border /ˈbɔːdə(r)/
charity work /ˈtʃærəti ˌwɜːk/
freedom /ˈfriːdəm/
gold medal /ˌgəʊld ˈmedl/
law /lɔː/
rainfall /ˈreɪnfɔːl/
scenery /ˈsiːnəri/
skateboarder /ˈskeɪtbɔːdə(r)/
snow /snəʊ/
snowboarder /ˈsnəʊbɔːdə(r)/
to be fond of doing something /tə ˌbi ˈfɒnd əv ˌduːɪŋ .../
to be good at doing something /tə ˌbi ˈgʊd ət ˌduːɪŋ .../
to be hopeless at doing something /tə ˌbi ˈhəʊpləs ət ˌduːɪŋ .../
to be interested in doing something /tə ˌbiː ˈɪntrəstɪd ɪn ˌduːɪŋ .../
to be keen on doing something /tə ˌbi ˈkiːn ɒn ˌduːɪŋ .../
to borrow /tə ˈbɒrəʊ/
to collect something /tə kəˈlekt .../
to compete /tə kəmˈpiːt/
to go off something /tə ˌgəʊ ˈɒf .../
to insist on doing something /tu ɪnˈsɪst ɒn ˌduːɪŋ .../
to look forward to doing something /tə ˌlʊk ˈfɔːwəd tə ˌduːɪŋ .../
to predict /tə prɪˈdɪkt/
to steal /tə ˈstiːl/

to think of doing something /tə 'θɪŋk əv ˌduːɪŋ .../
to win /tə 'wɪn/
unbelieveable /ʌnbɪ'liːvəbl/

Unit 10

a wooden box /ə ˌwʊdn 'bɒks/
bags of sugar /ˌbægz əv 'ʃʊɡə(r)/
bathroom taps /ˌbɑːθruːm 'tæps/
black market /ˌblæk 'mɑːkɪt/
comics /'kɒmɪks/
crazy /'kreɪzi/
exotic /ɪɡ'zɒtɪk/
factory /'fæktəri/
fascinated /'fæsɪneɪtɪd/
fascination /ˌfæsɪ'neɪʃn/
football pictures /'fʊtbɔːl ˌpɪktʃəz/
geology /dʒi'ɒlədʒi/
hometown /'həʊmtaʊn/
honeymoon /'hʌnimuːn/
microscope /'maɪkrəskəʊp/
model planes /ˌmɒdl 'pleɪnz/
packages /'pækɪdʒɪz/
sand /sænd/
shells /ʃelz/
souvenir /ˌsuːvə'nɪə(r)/
to be arrested /tə ˌbi əˈrestɪd/
to break the law /tə ˌbreɪk ðə 'lɔː/
to climb /tə 'klaɪm/
to collect things /tə kə'lekt ˌθɪŋz/
to do photography /tə ˌduː fə'tɒɡrəfi/
to do pottery /tə ˌduː 'pɒtəri/
to do puzzles /tə ˌduː 'pʌzlz/
to end /tu 'end/
to fall /tə 'fɔːl/
to fine someone /tə 'faɪn .../
to get help /tə ˌget 'help/
to go bird watching /tə ˌɡəʊ 'bɜːd ˌwɒtʃɪŋ/
to grow /tə 'ɡrəʊ/

to join /tə 'dʒɔɪn/
to keep /tə 'kiːp/
to keep a blog /tə ˌkiːp ə 'blɒɡ/
to lie in the sun /tə ˌlaɪ ɪn ðə 'sʌn/
to make models /tə ˌmeɪk 'mɒdlz/
to mend things /tə 'mend ˌθɪŋz/
to play online games /tə ˌpleɪ ɒnlaɪn 'ɡeɪmz/
to receive /tə rɪ'siːv/
to rent /tə 'rent/
to risk /tə 'rɪsk/
to search /tə 'sɜːtʃ/

Unit 11

animal testing /'ænɪml ˌtestɪŋ/
brave /breɪv/
demonstration /ˌdemən'streɪʃn/
determined /dɪ'tɜːmɪnd/
insensitive /ɪn'sensətɪv/
inspirational /ˌɪnspə'reɪʃənl/
intolerant /ɪn'tɒlərənt/
laboratories /lə'bɒrətriz/
limerick /'lɪmərɪk/
long distance /ˌlɒŋ 'dɪstəns/
miserable /'mɪzrəbl/
negative /'neɡətɪv/
outgoing /aʊt'ɡəʊɪŋ/
patient /'peɪʃnt/
readers /'riːdəz/
scared /skeəd/
selfish /'selfɪʃ/
sick /sɪk/
stupid /'stjuːpɪd/
syllable /'sɪləbl/
to accept /tu ək'sept/
to appreciate /tu ə'priːʃieɪt/
to bully /tə 'bʊli/
to cheer someone up /tə ˌtʃɪə ... 'ʌp/
to calm down /tə ˌkɑːm 'daʊn/
to crash /tə 'kræʃ/
to fit in /tə ˌfɪt 'ɪn/
to get angry /tə ˌɡet 'æŋɡri/

to get into fights /tə ˌɡet ˌɪntə 'faɪts/
to give someone bad marks /tə ˌɡɪv ... ˌbæd 'mɑːks/
to hang around with someone /tə 'hæŋ əˌraʊnd wɪð .../
to hate /tə 'heɪt/
to judge /tə 'dʒʌdʒ/
to laugh at someone /tə 'lɑːf ət .../
to leave school /tə ˌliːv 'skuːl/
to organise /tu 'ɔːɡənaɪz/
to pick on someone /tə 'pɪk ɒn .../
to share /tə 'ʃeə(r)/
to show someone something /tə 'ʃəʊ ... .../
to spread lies /tə ˌspred 'laɪz/
to take a long time /tə ˌteɪk ə ˌlɒŋ 'taɪm/
to tell someone off /tə ˌtel ... 'ɒf/
to treat someone badly /tə ˌtriːt ... 'bædli/
to whisper /tə 'wɪspə(r)/
to work things out /tə ˌwɜːk ˌθɪŋz 'aʊt/
tolerant /'tɒlərənt/
unadventurous /ˌʌnəd'ventʃərəs/

Unit 12

chemicals /'kemɪklz/
court /kɔːt/
daybreak /'deɪbreɪk/
fair price /ˌfeə 'praɪs/
farm /fɑːm/
fixed price /ˌfɪkst 'praɪs/
furious /'fjʊəriəs/
mine /maɪn/
pesticides /'pestɪsaɪdz/
prison /'prɪzn/
shade /ʃeɪd/
soup /suːp/
terrified /'terɪfaɪd/
to be fair/unfair /tə ˌbi 'feə(r), ʌn'feə(r)/
to beat someone /tə 'biːt .../

to care about /tə 'keər əˌbaʊt/
to cheat /tə 'tʃiːt/
to dig /tə 'dɪɡ/
to do experiments /tə ˌduː ɪk'sperɪmənts/
to earn money /tu ˌɜːn 'mʌni/
to fail a test /tə ˌfeɪl ə 'test/
to find /tə 'faɪnd/
to go to prison /tə ˌɡəʊ tə 'prɪzn/
to grow food /tə ˌɡrəʊ 'fuːd/
to have a crash /tə ˌhæv ə 'kræʃ/
to hear /tə 'hɪə(r)/
to knock on the door /tə ˌnɒk ɒn ðə 'dɔː(r)/
to lend /tə 'lend/
to pick something up /tə ˌpɪk ... 'ʌp/
to shout /tə 'ʃaʊt/
to steal /tə 'stiːl/
to store things /tə 'stɔː ˌθɪŋz/
to study hard /tə ˌstʌdi 'hɑːd/
to throw /tə 'θrəʊ/
to throw a stick /tə ˌθrəʊ ə 'stɪk/
to turn round /tə ˌtɜːn 'raʊnd/
to worry about something /tə 'wʌri əˌbaʊt .../
warden /'wɔːdn/
warehouse /'weəhaʊs/

Pronunciation guide

Vowels

/iː/	see
/ɪ/	bit
/e/	bed
/æ/	sad
/ɑː/	father
/ʌ/	cut
/ʊ/	cook
/uː/	too
/i/	happy
/ə/	above
/ɒ/	got
/ɔː/	saw
/u/	actual

Diphthongs

/ɜː/	circle
/eɪ/	say
/aɪ/	buy
/ɔɪ/	boy
/əʊ/	go
/aʊ/	now
/ɪə/	hear
/eə/	hair
/ʊə/	sure
/juː/	few
/aɪə/	fire
/aʊə/	power

Consonants

/p/	push
/b/	bank
/t/	time
/d/	diary
/k/	carpet
/g/	big
/f/	surf
/v/	very
/θ/	thin
/ð/	that
/s/	sit
/z/	zero
/ʃ/	shine
/ʒ/	measure
/h/	hot
/w/	water
/tʃ/	chair
/dʒ/	joke
/m/	more
/n/	snow
/ŋ/	sing
/r/	ring
/l/	small
/j/	you

CAMBRIDGE UNIVERSITY PRESS
www.cambridge.org/elt

HELBLING LANGUAGES
www.helblinglanguages.com

More! 4 Student's Book
by Herbert Puchta & Jeff Stranks
with G. Gerngross C. Holzmann P. Lewis-Jones

© Cambridge University Press and Helbling Languages 2009
(*More* was originally published by Helbling Languages © Helbling Languages 2006)

All rights reserved. No part of this publication may be reproduced, stored in a retrieval system, or transmitted, in any form or by any means, electronic, mechanical, photocopying, recording, or otherwise, without the prior written permission of the Publishers.

First published 2009
5th printing 2012

Printed in Italy by L.E.G.O. S.p.A.

A catalogue record for this publication is available from the British Library

ISBN	Title
978-0-521-71314-6	More! 4 Student's Book with interactive CD-ROM
978-0-521-71315-3	More! 4 Workbook with Audio CD
978-0-521-71316-0	More! 4 Teacher's Book
978-0-521-71318-4	More! 4 Teacher's Resource Pack with Testbuilder CD-ROM/Audio CD
978-0-521-71320-7	More! 4 Class Audio CDs
978-0-521-71319-1	More! 4 Extra Practice Book
978-0-521-71321-4	More! 4 DVD (PAL/NTSC)

The authors would like to thank those people who have made significant contributions towards the final form of MORE! INTERNATIONAL:

Oonagh Wade and Rosamund Cantalamessa for their expertise in working on the manuscripts, their useful suggestions for improvement, and the support we got from them.

Lucia Astuti and Markus Spielmann, Helbling Languages, Ron Ragsdale and James Dingle, Cambridge University Press, for their dedication to the project and innovative publishing vision.

Our designers, Amanda Hockin, Greg Sweetnam, Quantico, Craig Cornell and Niels Gyde for their imaginative layouts and stimulating creativity. Also, our artwork assistants, Silvia Scorzoso and Francesca Gironi, for their dedicated work.

The publisher would like to thank the following for their kind permission to reproduce the following photograph and other copyright material:

Alamy p6 (Rugby shirt; basketball boots), p9, p10, p12, p22, p34 (dancer), p35, p37, p39, p42, p43, p45 (CD: Food Icon; pizza), p49, p52, p54, p56 (tennis tournament; book fair; school fete), p59 (Rolling Stones; samba school), p60, p66 (CD: Food Icon; baked potato), p69, p70 (CD: Food Icons; CD: Ultimate Food), p72, p73, p80, p82 (human statue), p86, p89, p90, p93, p96 (blog; coins; mending bicycle; making models), p99 (badges), p114, p116 (miner; prison warden; porter), p123; book cover of A Step from Heaven by An Na (Front Street, an imprint of **Boyds Mills Press, Inc.** , 2001) p46; **Corbis** p13, p31, p73 (Take That), p90 (Shaun White); **Getty Images** p10 (Manchester Stadium), p56 (opening night), p60 (logo of Wimbledon), p63, p69 (Jamie Oliver), p72 (Oasis), p73 (The Chemical Brothers), p79 (Walter Raleigh), p86 (Cars), p90 (Prince Harry), p122; **Andy Hay (rspb-images.com)** p103; **The International Sand Collector Society, Nick D'Errico** ISCS/PG Director p94; ©**iStockphoto.com** p6 (gloves), p33, p34, p40, p53 (terns), p59, p103 (golden eagle), p116 (aerobic teacher); **NASA, NSSDC** p14; **Penguin Groups Ltd** front cover of Half moon investigation by Eoin Colfer (Puffin 2006) p46; **PlanetSpace** p19 (Canadian Arrow); **Railway Cat Creations** front cover of The Hunter and the Hunted by Al Wilde, p46; jacket cover from THE CURIOUS INCIDENT OF THE DOG IN THE NIGHT-TIME by Mark Haddon. Used by permission of Doubleday, a division of **Random House, Inc.** p46; book cover of THE LOST ART by Simon Morden, reprinted by permission of **The Random House Group Ltd** p46; **Reuters** p30; **Shutterstock** p6, p10 (volleyball; cricket), p12 (turkey; corn), p14, p26, p32, p35 (vet; boy; girl), p37 (ballet dancer; boy holding books), p39 (York), p43 (omelette), p45, p53, p56, p62, p63 (girl), p66, p69 (junk food), p70 (spinach; cabbage; coffee; pineapple; hamburger; chocolate), p71, p74, p79, p82, p85, p92, p94 (sand), p96, p99, p102, p103, p105, p109, p116; Cover design © 2007 Walker Books Ltd. Boy with torch Logo™ & Alex Rider™ & © 2007 Stormbreaker Productions Ltd. From SNAKEHEAD by Anthony Horowitz Reproduced by permission of **Walker Books Ltd**, London SE11 5HJ, p49.

The publishers would like to thank the following illustrators:
Roberto Battestini, Pietro Dichiara, Michele Farella, Björn Pertoft, Lucilla Stellato,

The publishers would like to thank the following for their assistance with commissioned photographs:
David Tolley Ltd. pp 4, 24, 44, 64, 84, 104
Studio Antonietti pp 15, 74, 75, 76, 77,

We would also like to thank **Bonnie, Costa Coffee, Jee Saheb** and **Elmer Cotton Sports** of Oxford for their help with locations and props for the photostory.